# Matrimonial Finance Toolkit

SECOND EDITION

## Related titles from Law Society Publishing:

**Children Law Handbook**
Safda Mahmood

**Cohabitation**
Stephen Parker

**Divorce, Dissolution and Separation**
David Burrows

**Matrimonial Finance Handbook**
Mena Ruparel

**Open Justice and Privacy in Family Proceedings**
David Burrows

**Social Care Charging**
Arianna Kelly

**Special Guardianship and Adoption Handbook**
Safda Mahmood

# Matrimonial Finance Toolkit

SECOND EDITION

Mena Ruparel and Karen Dovaston

The Law Society

**Purchasers of this book who sign up to My LS can access a free download of individual Word and Excel files containing precedent policies, letters and checklists. This is hosted on the Law Society Learning platform which offers a range of courses.** To access the download page set up for this book, go to **https://learn.lawsociety.org.uk/product/matrimonial-finance-toolkit**, and add this to your Law Society Learning account just as you would add a course. Select the 'I have a multipass' option and enter the code: **UPGW7638**. You will be taken to a download page: click 'Start' to download a .zip file. If you need some help with My LS contact our helpline on 020 7242 1222.



ISBN 978-1-78446-201-7

First edition published in 2017
This second edition published in 2024 by the Law Society
113 Chancery Lane, London WC2A 1PL

Typeset by IDS Infotech Ltd
Printed by Hobbs the Printers Ltd, Totton, Hants

The paper used for the text pages of this book is FSC® certified. FSC (the Forest Stewardship Council®) is an international network to promote responsible management of the world's forests.

MIX
Paper | Supporting responsible forestry
FSC® C020438

# Contents

# About the authors

**Mena Ruparel** is a member of the King's Counsel Appointments panel and an Independent Complaints Assessor for the Department for Transport. She spent more than 20 years as a specialist family law solicitor, during which time she was also an examiner, lecturer and author of family law and ethics books.

**Karen Dovaston** has specialised in family law since qualifying as a solicitor in 1995. She is Chair of the Law Society's Family Law Committee, Vice Chair of the Forum of Family Arbitrators, assessor for the Law Society's Family Law Microcredential and Law Society Council member for Essex from 2024. She has appeared on television, radio, and commented in various media publications.

# Preface to the first edition

When I qualified as a solicitor I used a book similar to this to get me through the drafting issues that faced me daily. The Form E was introduced about a year after I qualified and all practitioners had to get to grips with the intricacies of the form and the preparation of the new questionnaire and statement of issues. It was a very different way of working as previously we had been drafting freehand, which is now almost unheard of. The way that these documents are drafted today is quite different from the way that they were drafted then.

It is my hope that practitioners will find this toolkit useful as it contains many practical precedents to get matrimonial practitioners through the week without tearing their hair out. Even experienced practitioners are plagued by preparing letters of instruction to single joint experts and so I have provided four precedents that should cover every base.

I would like to thank a number of fellow practitioners for their assistance in checking that these precedents are fit for purpose. Lewis Hulatt of Major Family Law has been a great help in going through the precedents and suggesting helpful amendments. Thanks also to Roopa Ahluwalia of Birketts solicitors, Karen Dovaston of Jefferies solicitors and Melanie Barnes of Major Family Law for their input.

Mark Penston of Bluesky chartered financial planners has helped with the tricky pensions sections of the Form E, the section on how to explain pensions to a client and the drafting of the single joint expert's letter at Annex 4D. Mark has been my 'go to' person for expertise on pensions for 10 years and I am grateful to him for his continued assistance.

I am aware that there are more practitioners than ever before moving into the field of matrimonial finance from other areas of law which are no longer financially viable. I hope that this toolkit will become a useful staple for their flourishing practices.

Mena Ruparel
July 2017

# Preface to the second edition

A significant part of the job of being a solicitor, particularly in the area of family law, revolves around communication; from the lack of it between our clients to the effective communication from us to our clients. In family law, our clients are often asked to make really big decisions at a time when they are, arguably, at their lowest in terms of emotional strength to be able to do that. The job of the solicitor is to help them and guide them through, directing them to therapists, life coaches, counsellors, accountants, financial advisers to name a few, who can also give guidance and support.

I am, and always have been, a proponent of using plain English. Yes, you know long, clever words and you are clever, working in this area. Take that as a given and do not use correspondence to show off that. Use it to communicate to your client in a way that makes sense to them. Correspondence may also not be the most effective way to communicate either. The 'tone of voice' you sent your email in may not be the 'tone of voice' it is read in. Also, listen. We have two ears, two eyes and one mouth. Think about dividing their use in that proportion.

I have always had books like this in my 'library'. Perhaps you have no templates at all or perhaps you want to tweak and improve yours. Templates are to be used and tinkered with. Use them as effective communication tools and don't forget to check them over once every six to 12 months at least.

And now the thanks. Thanks to my good friend, Mena Ruparel, for handing the baton on to me to update her original work to this edition. Thanks also to my husband, who supports me practically living in my home office at the end of the garden.

Karen Dovaston
July 2024

# A note about the templates in this book

## Letters to your clients

I am firmly of the view that a precedent should be used as a tool and not a rule. For many of the precedents here, you can put them in letter format or you can convert them to a leaflet (my personal favourite) to send to a client.

If you think the wording does not suit your style, tinker with it. I also advocate that you look through all of your precedents and template letters every six to 12 months just to make sure you still need them, that they are still accurate and they are in the right tone of voice.

Remember, the whole purpose of the letter or the leaflet is to explain things to your client. Clear, plain English and no jargon is a must. Clients are navigating a whole new world with you as their guide. Be a good, patient one.

## Court documentation

In a digital platform, it is easy to forget the formalities required in preparing your documentation; however, the formalities are important. The first thing the judge will see about you and your handling of the case is how you have prepared your documentation.

Make sure you know the court rules for the format of your documents – 3 cm margins, 12 point font and 1.5 line spacing, with each page numbered at the bottom.

Refresh your memory of the requirements for presentation of exhibits. Multiple documents are to be collated into a consecutively paginated, indexed bundle. This is particularly so for your Form E documents.

Remember that Replies must be verified by a statement of truth.

I have been preparing court bundles for longer than I am willing to admit but I still always have Practice Direction 27A open, just to remind me. You are not expected to remember everything but you are expected to know when and where to look for things.

The suite of standard orders can be found on the judiciary website (**www.judiciary.uk**).

The letter of instruction for a pension expert can be found in the Pension Advisory Group report, 'A Guide to the Treatment of Pensions on Divorce' (Second Edition, 2024). This can be downloaded free of charge from the Nuffield Foundation website (**www.nuffieldfoundation.org**).

# Abbreviations

| | |
|---|---|
| CAA | Case Access Administrator |
| CE | cash equivalent |
| CEV | cash equivalent value |
| CGT | Capital Gains Tax |
| CMS | Child Maintenance Service |
| CPI | Consumer Price Index |
| CSA | Child Support Agency |
| FDA | first directions appointment (First Appointment) |
| FDR | financial dispute resolution |
| FPR 2010 | Family Procedure Rules 2010, SI 2010/2955 |
| FRWG | Financial Remedies Working Group |
| MCA 1973 | Matrimonial Causes Act 1973 |
| MIAM | mediation information and assessment meeting |
| NCDR | non-court dispute resolution |
| PBA | Payment By Account |
| PODE | pension on divorce expert |
| PPF | Pension Protection Fund |
| PPR | principal primary residence |
| PRPA | person responsible for the pension arrangement |
| RPI | Retail Price Index |
| SRA | Solicitors Regulation Authority |

# 1 From the beginning

## 1.1 Arranging the first meeting

### *1.1.1 The format of the meeting*

The world that we live in now, after the Covid-19 pandemic declared in March 2020, is much changed. Previously nearly all of the meetings between a solicitor and their client would have been face to face. Some international practices and others at the forefront of technology may well have been using remote or video conferencing, but generally the legal sphere seemed almost untouched by the effective use of technology.

Post Covid lockdowns, we have moved a long way from the traditional model of solicitor/client/office. When a potential client makes contact, your first consideration will be what format the initial meeting will take. Remote/video hearings can work well in the family sphere, with positive aspects such as convenience for the client and the solicitor, opening up different hours of availability, allowing for different costing models and so on. There remains a place for the face-to-face meeting, but you should not shy away from embracing new technology and advancements.

### *1.1.2 The type of meeting*

The initial meeting will largely depend on what your firm offers, or what you decide to offer. Some firms offer 15 minutes or 30 minutes without charge. Others offer a fixed fee first session, often for a reduced rate. Yet others simply aim for charging per time spent. Many firms will have a 'pay in advance' fixed- or agreed-fee initial advice session; others will have a 'pay on the day' policy.

Your firm may be offering the one solicitor/one couple model where you are dealing with both parties to the marriage/civil partnership.

The key is to be clear what you are offering your prospective client, how much it will cost, when you expect payment and what it will cover.

It is important to note that the acceptance of money for fees does not fall within the scope of the Money Laundering, Terrorist Financing and Transfer of Funds (Information on the Payer) Regulations 2017, SI 2017/692 (as amended). Until the change to the Money Laundering Regulations in January 2020, most family law solicitors were outside the scope of the Regulations, only being brought within on account of securing tax advice for clients. Your firm may have technology to deal with the identification of your client before your first meeting, and there are several apps/software options in the market place for this. If your firm uses this approach, make sure to tell your client before the first meeting that you will be making this check as it may appear on their credit record.

### *1.1.3 Obtaining information prior to your meeting*

Prior to recent advancements in technology, most of your information from a client would be taken in the initial meeting. There are disadvantages to this in that often the client will be nervous, feel as if they are taking an exam and may not have the information to hand.

From your perspective, you are dealing with the 'admin' of taking names and addresses, which is eating into the time the client has with you, and you are also having to assimilate information at a fast pace.

There are several solutions to this mischief. For example, there are software solutions that provide for 'onboarding' a client, allowing them to input their data from the comfort of their own home in advance of the meeting with you, so that each of you has time to consider and assimilate this information. Use this to your advantage and think about what you want to know from your client. The first sections of the initial meeting note at **Annex 1A** are some examples. You may have others.

## 1.2 The content of the meeting

### *1.2.1 What regulatory/client care matters must be covered*

There are basic formalities for all of your meetings. You will need to:

1. have a note for your file of all of the information given to you;
2. have a note for your file of the information and advice given by you to your client;
3. at the end of the meeting, unless sent before, provide your client care letter, terms and conditions of business and confirmation of any advice given.

It is suggested that, whilst seemingly still loved by practitioners, clients are not over enamoured with lengthy, wordy letters. It is suggested that your client care letter could be no more than one page, with terms and conditions of business in a separate document referenced as an enclosure, along with a copy of your file note, setting out information given by the client and advice given by you.

An example of an initial meeting note is in **Annex 1A**. Whilst on the topic of templates, the use of a template is a tool not a rule and you would be wise to review all of your templates at least every six months to check for tone of voice, updates in the law or practice and generally to 'tinker' with them to address the needs of your clients. The templates offered in this book are not sacrosanct – amend them if you think it is helpful.

It is most likely that you will be sending information and advice to your client via email. Your firm may have security software on outbound emails; however, it is good practice to warn your client of the possibility of interception and that they should regularly change all of their passwords across all email, banking and social networks so as to protect their data.

### *1.2.2 The likely areas in which you will advise*

There are some common themes that repeat in the initial advice session. They are as follows and the list is not exhaustive:

- Divorce and finance are linked jurisdictionally but dealt with in 'silos'.
- Divorce ends the marriage but not the financial connection.
- The right to make financial claims can still remain live after divorce.
- The financial connection can only be terminated by an order and you can only have such an order if there are divorce proceedings at conditional order stage.
- Not all cases are decided by the judge and most settle.
- The types of financial orders that can be made and the limitations.
- The need for financial disclosure and what that means.
- The difference between matrimonial and non-matrimonial assets.
- The factors to be considered in the Matrimonial Causes Act (MCA) 1973, s.25.
- An explanation that the court will take a broad-brush approach and there will not be a forensic accounting of the marriage.
- Finances are not used to 'punish' either partner.
- Meeting 'need' in the sense of the legal term is often the beginning and the end if assets are limited.

Remember your job is not to recite the law but to explain in practical and plain terms to your client what issues they are likely to have to tackle. Be clear with your client that you will not be telling them what to do – instead, you will be working in partnership with them and advising them of options, and you may have to ask for the advice/expertise of others because there are limits to the advice you can give. It is recommended that you familiarise yourself with the Language Matters project from the Family Solutions Group, the Good Practice Guide to Correspondence from Resolution and the Law Society's Family Law Protocol. All give guidance as to the best way to communicate with your client, particularly in writing, which has its own limitations.

For example, you may need to get a property valued. You may need tax advice for your client. You no doubt have a basic understanding of the taxation regime if you are working in financial cases but you cannot give this advice to the client and the same applies to financial advice. As a solicitor, you are not regulated to give financial advice so be careful not to stray into that area. It is an offence under the Financial Services and Markets Act 2000 to do so.

Pay attention to pension assets. These are complex and often very valuable assets. Familiarise yourself with the report of the Pension Advisory Group, 'A Guide to the

Treatment of Pensions on Divorce' (Second Edition, 2024), which is available for download free of charge from the Nuffield Foundation website (**www.nuffieldfoundation.org**). There is a guide for the client in plain English available for free download from the Advicenow website (**www.advicenow.org.uk**). In particular, consider whether your client is likely to need a report from a pension on divorce expert (PODE), as referred to in the Pension Advisory Group report.

### *1.2.3 Out-of-court dispute resolution*

The Law Society's Family Law Protocol (Fourth Edition) reminds you that you should consider all alternatives for dispute resolution with your client, not just court applications. You should explain to your client that for financial matters, the aim is to try to reach agreement if you can, and the various routes that can be taken to get to that agreement, including discussions between your client and their spouse, mediation, the collaborative process, Early Neutral Evaluation within mediation, solicitor-involved mediation, private financial dispute resolution (FDR) and also arbitration – with any combination of any process being possible.

A model gaining traction is the 'one solicitor/one couple' model of varying names but essentially this is a model where one solicitor is working for both parties to the marriage. Of course, if you have already seen one party without the other being present or engaged that could mean that you cannot be the 'one solicitor' in that model but you should still explain it to your client.

There are various labels for various processes but the key is to consider what it is that you are trying to achieve for your client, and the best method of doing that. It could be a simple Zoom meeting with each client in their own room, and you and the other representative speaking in a third room on a without prejudice basis that will help parties come to an agreement. Be creative. Check your regulatory obligations via the SRA website (**www.sra.org.uk**).

### *1.2.4 Limitations to advice in the first session with your client*

Your client will no doubt want to have advice as to what to do/likely outcomes and may expect to get that at the first meeting. This is very common in financial cases. Do not be afraid to tell your client you do not know and you need to research the answer to a question, or that this is your initial view/indication but that this might change as matters unroll. You simply need to explain this to your client, to limit their expectations. Finances are complex matters and financial disclosure may uncover all kinds of hidden considerations. You are not obliged to guess at an answer and you should not do that. It is unfair to the client who places reliance on your response and it is unfair to yourself, as you may feel anxiety over having done so, particularly where the information you will have been given will undoubtedly be unverified and patchy.

Make sure your client is aware of the general process, the time that can take, how things can change with cases being decided by the court all the time, changes in the markets, changes in property prices and so on. The aim is for your client to understand that you have no control over these factors and this could be a reason why your advice may change at a later date.

### *1.2.5 Examples of issues that may require attention in the immediate term*

#### Litigants in person applying for a divorce

Many of your clients may be undertaking the divorce proceedings themselves, given the development of the digital divorce portal specifically for use by litigants in person. It is important to remind them that the email notifications they receive are not the orders, and so they need to log in to download the orders – particularly the conditional order, because you will not be able to lodge an application for an order by consent without it.

#### Applications to make the final divorce order or to prevent it being made

On the topic of divorce applications, you should consider whether your client needs advice regarding an application to stop the final divorce order being made (if the respondent) or simply needs to be told not to apply to finalise the divorce until the financial matters have been resolved, so as to protect pension rights and all options when being fully engaged in making and responding to financial applications. This is particularly important if your client is considering a remarriage.

If you are advising the respondent, consider asking the applicant for an undertaking not to apply for the final divorce order until the financial orders are made or for sufficient notice to be given to you before such an application is made. This may avoid the need to make a formal application to prohibit the order.

#### Home rights and registering a notice to protect

Another area that generally requires an immediate consideration is that relating to the family home. If the home is in the name of the other party, you should advise your client on early registration of a Home Rights Notice, now quickly done via the HM Land Registry portal in a matter of minutes.

#### Severing the joint tenancy in respect of a property

If the property is in joint names, you may need to consider the benefits of severance of the beneficial joint tenancy and making a short 'holding' Will while financial matters are being resolved.

It is worth your while to become conversant with the HM Land Registry portal which can be used for obtaining office copy entries (current and historic); copies of documents (transfers, restrictions and so on); making applications for Home Rights Notices; and registering a restriction in form RX1 if the property is not the family home but your client has a financial/prospective financial interest.

## The 'bank of Mum and Dad'

Frequently, there may have been a contribution from a parent(s) towards the purchase of property or towards legal fees. You need to take careful instructions from your client about such contributions. Was it a gift or a loan? Was it recorded in writing? How was it paid? Is it being repaid? Familiarise yourself also with the case law regarding 'soft' loans – i.e. loans from a non-commercial outfit.

## Small companies

Very often, a small limited company will have been set up either by one of the spouses or jointly as a vehicle for one spouse to earn an income. For example, a tradesperson such as a plumber who would be self employed, but for tax/liability reasons has formed a limited company, appointed themselves and their spouse as directors and allocated equal shareholdings to both. This is often done without a shareholder agreement in place. Companies House will give you much information but there will be more needed, generally from the company's accountant. There is usually one spouse who is the dominant earner in such a venture and the other spouse has been employed or appointed for tax efficiency reasons. It is very important that one spouse does not attempt to dismiss/fire the other, whether overtly or by locking them out of accounts and so on. Such action can lead to employment claims and damages awarded. The best option is to get advice from an employment law specialist and to get information from the accountant about the company structure.

## Communication and social media

It is strongly recommended that you tell your clients to resist the temptation of posting on social media about the shortcomings of the other spouse, or indeed anything to do with the financial divorce or children matters. Not only can it come back to them as an issue but also the forums are open to other adults and even to the children of the parties, whether they may have accounts at the time or later join. Imagine a young teenager seeing the details of their parents' separation all over Facebook. This is to be avoided.

Similarly, your client should be warned away from iMessages, WhatsApp, text messages and similar messaging services. They are too quick to send – not enough time between brain, emotion, fingers and sending – and they can be edited after the message has been sent. If communication is at an all time low, consider using a communication App built for separating families. OurFamilyWizard and AppClose seem to be the market leaders at present.

## Smash and grab

If both parties are still living in the same house, and your client may know or be able to guess the other party's passwords, remember to advise them not to access the other party's electronic devices or accounts and not to search through or remove paperwork belonging to the other party. The case law is clear on this.

### 1.2.6 *Marital agreements and deeds of trust*

Marital agreements and deeds of trust are becoming more common so you should remember to ask about them at the first meeting. They may have significant impact on the advice that will be given. Ask not only about the terms of the agreement but also the circumstances surrounding the making of such an agreement. Who drafted it? Did each have legal advice? Is your client clear on the terms and still happy with the terms?

It is wise to ask also about contributions to the purchase of property and the asset base – if only to give rounded advice, consider possible intervenors and to avoid surprises later on.

### 1.2.7 *Letters and leaflets*

Your role is to impart the information to your clients in an effective way, without legal jargon, to ensure they understand their options, the process and your advice.

You can do that in letter format – but consider the state of mind of your client as you do this. This area is your 'day to day' but it will not be for them. Overlay the stress, emotion and fear of the future they may be facing. There is a limit to the volume of information your client will be able to digest. Avoid the temptation to give them everything all at once.

It is a personal preference, however, the author's view is that long letters can be very off-putting for a client and the better option for them would be to have a short letter with a leaflet enclosed. **Annexes 1B** to **1M** give examples.

Depending on what service your firm is offering to the client, the initial advice note may simply be a reiteration of basic advice and information with headline notes pertaining to the client's particular situation. Your leaflets can be rolled out to your client piece by piece to give them time to assimilate the information.

# Annex 1A

## Note of initial advice session

| | |
|---|---|
| Date | |
| Venue | |
| With | |

| **Details of the parties** | |
|---|---|
| Client name | |
| Client address | |
| Client date of birth | |
| Other party is | |
| Date of birth | |
| Address | |

| | |
|---|---|
| Marriage date | |
| Cohab before marriage | |
| Date of separation | |

| **Children's names** | **Date of birth** | **School** |
|---|---|---|
| | | |
| | | |
| Arrangements for children seeing both parents | | |

| **The former family home** | |
|---|---|
| Address | |
| Type of property | |
| Bought on | |
| At a cost of | |
| Funded by | |
| Value now | |
| Mortgage balance | |
| Mortgage with | |
| Type of mortgage | Repayment/interest only |
| Monthly payment | |
| Paid by | |
| Occupied by | |
| Any arrears? | No/Yes £ |
| **Any other property** | |
| Neither has any property other than the former family home | |

| **Bank accounts** | |
|---|---|
| Joint accounts | |
| Sole name accounts | |
| **Savings/shares/collections/cars/investments/inheritances/injury claims** | |
| Mrs | |
| Mr | |
| **Debts** | |
| Mrs | |
| Mr | |
| **Pensions:** | |
| Mrs | |
| Mr | |
| **Income: Mrs** | |
| Occupation | |
| Employed/self employed | |
| Hours worked each week | |
| Gross pay | |
| Net monthly pay | |
| Child benefit | |
| WTC/CTC/UC | |
| Maintenance | |
| **Income: Mr** | |
| Occupation | |
| Employed/self employed | |
| Hours worked each week | |
| Gross pay | |
| Net monthly pay | |
| Child benefit | |
| WTC/CTC/UC | |
| Maintenance | |

| **Why separate?** |
|---|
| |
| **Some things to consider based on the facts given to me were:** |
| |

**Advice given**

***Divorce or not***

Most people are looking for the marriage to be brought to an end and also for the financial relationship and connection to be brought to an end. You can only get a financial order if you start divorce proceedings. If people are not ready to start divorce proceedings, you can deal with the finances by putting an agreement into a Separation Agreement but:

1. It has to be by agreement and written up.
2. It cannot be used to share pensions – you have to have an order for that.
3. It can be overridden by the court when divorce and financial proceedings are to be sorted out but those situations are rare.
4. Both of you have to give financial disclosure to the other and this is listed in the document itself, i.e. you tell each other what you have.
5. It has to be 'fair' within the court view of what is fair at the time it is considered – so there is some risk in guessing what 'fair' might look like in the future.
6. Both of you have to have legal advice.

**Basic rule:** Do not sign off on these unless you want and expect to be held to the terms and unless the agreement you reach would be considered fair or endorsed by the court, there is little point in having a Separation Agreement drawn up because in the event of a dispute, the other party would have good grounds for challenge.

***Divorce***

**Grounds for divorce:** The only requirements in an application for a divorce are for you to confirm:

1. that the marriage is irretrievably broken down; and
2. that you want to be divorced.

**Digital system:** Proceedings should be started in the digital portal system as this is faster.

**Applications:** Can be made by one spouse (sole applicant) or by both spouses together (joint application). One solicitor can act for both parties as joint applicants – but not yet using the digital system; only the slower papers system. If you apply as a sole applicant, the papers still have to be sent to the other spouse.

**Defending/disputing a divorce:** This is now called 'disputing a divorce'. This can only be done if there is a dispute about:

1. whether there was a valid marriage ceremony;
2. whether the court in England and Wales has jurisdiction to deal with the divorce.

**Divorce orders:** These still come in two parts: a conditional order (and you remain married) and the final order (and you will be divorced).

**Timing:** The earliest that a conditional order can be applied for is 20 weeks from the date that the divorce application was started. After a conditional order is made, a final order can be made after a further wait period of 6 weeks and 1 day.

**Finances:** Divorce does not deal with financial matters or arrangements for children. You should not finalise a divorce until the financial matters have been agreed and resolved by way of a court order.

It usually takes 6 months for a divorce to be finalised depending on whether your spouse co-operates. Sometimes, it is best not to finalise the divorce until the financial matters are sorted out. If your original marriage certificate is not in English, it has to be translated by a professional translator.

**New law:** This came into effect on 6 April 2022 to bring sweeping changes to divorce law. The application still is made to the court via the digital portal but you can have joint applications as well as sole applications. The old 'grounds' are swept away to be replaced by a simple statement that the marriage is over and you want a divorce. This is called 'no fault divorce'. Hopefully, it will help to reduce tensions when getting divorced. The downside is that there is a mandatory 20 week wait before a divorce can be finalised.

**Fees:** The court fee is [£X], whether it is a sole or joint application. Our costs for a solicitor managed divorce from start to end are [£X] + VAT ([£X]). The total cost if we deal with the divorce for you is [£X]. There is very limited provision for one party to ask the other to pay their legal costs of divorce and the new law provides for each party to pay their own costs to be the standard. This means if you want a contribution from your spouse towards the costs of a divorce, this should be asked for before the divorce is started.

***Financial matters***

Divorce and finance are linked but the best way to explain the relationship is as train tracks. The divorce 'track' starts first and then when the application has got to a certain point, the financial 'track' is unlocked so that if the parties have been unable to reach an agreement then they have the option of making an application to the court and for the judge to decide for them.

Alternatively, if they have reached an agreement then that can be turned into the form of an order and presented to the court to ask them to make the order. This is not a 'rubber stamp' exercise and the judge can refuse to approve the order.

**The aim is to try to reach an agreement, if at all possible.** In practical terms, what usually happens is that the divorce is started off and whilst that is progressing, the parties are working in the background to try to get to the point of an agreement in respect of the finances, so both things are happening at the same time. If the parties can reach an agreement, we can turn it into a court order and we can offer a fixed fee for that.

Most people who came to ask about financial matters wanted to know how the finances would be divided.

There are no absolute answers and our law gives a large element of discretion. There may be a number of 'right' solutions.

A **first consideration** would be to try to end the financial relationship if possible. A second consideration would be for any children under the age of 18 and their housing needs. Both parents will remain financially responsible for their children and no obligation in that respect can be stopped by orders made between the parties to the marriage.

The **scope of the financial assets** needs to be clarified first of all. Then there is a consideration of what are matrimonial assets built up during the course of the marriage and what are non-matrimonial assets. The most common example of a non-matrimonial asset would be an inheritance. For most cases, the assets are not large enough to meet both parties' needs so non-matrimonial assets usually have to be used.

There is then a consideration of entitlement to the assets built up during the marriage and a consideration of what each of your financial needs are covering housing, income and pension in basic areas.

There are some **basic principles** that apply in all cases, however, and these can be summarised in a basic form as follows:

1. If you have children, one of the first concerns will be about housing for the children. It is not the overriding or only concern but it can be important.
2. If possible, the aim is to achieve a final settlement without continuing obligations towards each other so that you can move on with your lives. In a case with limited money, it can mean looking at meeting the needs of the parent with care of a child.
3. It is about fairness, so that you each take an equal drop in lifestyle and the presumption for the starting point for sharing assets is that you have equal shares. There are some factors that can change this but this depends on your circumstances.
4. Consideration is given to what you earn or could earn. This might mean you would be expected to get a job if you do not have one or re-train to be suitable for a different job if you cannot get work in your preferred area of employment.

5. All assets are considered but some can be treated differently to others, such as inheritances or money you had and kept separate before you married. The family home is always treated as a family asset but this does not mean it has to be shared equally. It does not matter in whose name the asset is held. Assets accrued during the course of the marriage are all put into the 'pot' available for sharing.
6. Health, age and disability can sometimes affect a settlement.
7. Child maintenance is not dealt with by the court. If you can't reach agreement, you need to apply to the Child Maintenance Service (CMS) for them to assess child maintenance. If you do reach agreement, it can be recorded in an order but you are only bound by it for one year and then after that either one of you can make an application to the CMS for a child maintenance calculation. The part of the order dealing with child maintenance is then brought to an end. If you are very wealthy and earn more than £156,000 gross per annum, the court can order top-up child maintenance.
8. Pensions are relevant, whether state, private or employer pensions. Pensions can be very valuable. They are not the same as money in the bank, however, and cannot be drawn upon until you reach at least the age of 55.

The **types of orders** that can be made are:

1. Payments from one spouse to another (periodical payments orders – not the same as child maintenance).
2. Capital orders – lump sums, transfers of shares, transfers of ISAs.
3. Property transfer orders – transfer of the property from one spouse to the other.
4. Property sale orders – an order for the property to be sold.
5. Pension sharing orders or pension attachment orders.

Child maintenance is usually dealt with by agreement or as assessed by the CMS. The court cannot deal with child maintenance unless the parent who does not live with the child earns more than £156,000 gross per annum. The court can order 'top up' maintenance on top of regular child maintenance for high earners.

***Making a temporary Will***

If you own a property with your spouse, you might want to consider making a temporary Will whilst your divorce and financial matters are being resolved. We would recommend checking how you are holding the property as owners – beneficial joint tenants means on your death the property goes to your co-owner, irrespective of what is in your Will. If you don't want that then we can help you change that arrangement and make a temporary Will.

***Mediation***

There is the option of mediation, which would give a place for the parties to discuss the financial matters in the presence of an independent third party.

Mediation has to be considered before making an application to the court and a Mediation Information and Assessment Meeting (MIAM) has to be attended, either in person or via a remote video session. The court rules changed on 29 April 2024 to give more force to the requirement that parties try to mediate or use another non-court dispute resolution option (NCDR) to resolve their arrangements outside of the court arena. The court has the option of pausing court proceedings to allow parties to go away and consider mediation. You will be required to give a statement before the first court hearing, and likely before each court hearing, to set out your position as to whether you are willing to use NCDR and if not, why not. The aim is to reduce the need for judicial intervention and to encourage parties to resolve their own issues, with legal advice if they need or want it.

The mediator can work with the parties to help them to exchange financial information and to discuss what they each want or the exchange of financial information can be done via solicitors.

| |
|---|
| The mediator will not give legal advice but they can come back to us in between mediation sessions if they need to. Negotiations/discussions can be done via solicitors. This work would be charged on an hourly rate, depending on what needs to be done. Mediation can be used in conjunction with solicitors or solicitors themselves can arrange a round table meeting. You could also have an Early Neutral Evaluation arranged via a mediator where an experienced solicitor/arbitrator is given the information about you and gives a non-binding indication based on that information of what a court would consider doing. |
| ***Arbitration*** |
| If parties cannot agree all the issues between them, they can jointly appoint an independent arbitrator who will decide the issues they submit for decision and adopt the format or process the parties agree.<br><br>For example, they could ask for a paper-based assessment only on agreed figures and only on some of the issues, the others having been agreed. Arbitration has the benefit of being binding, fast, confidential, flexible and usually a lower cost than court proceedings. |

# Annex 1B

## Financial remedies and how it works

We aim to try to negotiate an agreement in relation to financial matters between you and your husband/wife. This is because it is cheaper and faster for you. There are a number of ways to get to the point of an agreement; however, if you cannot get to an agreement, the Court will decide what should happen.

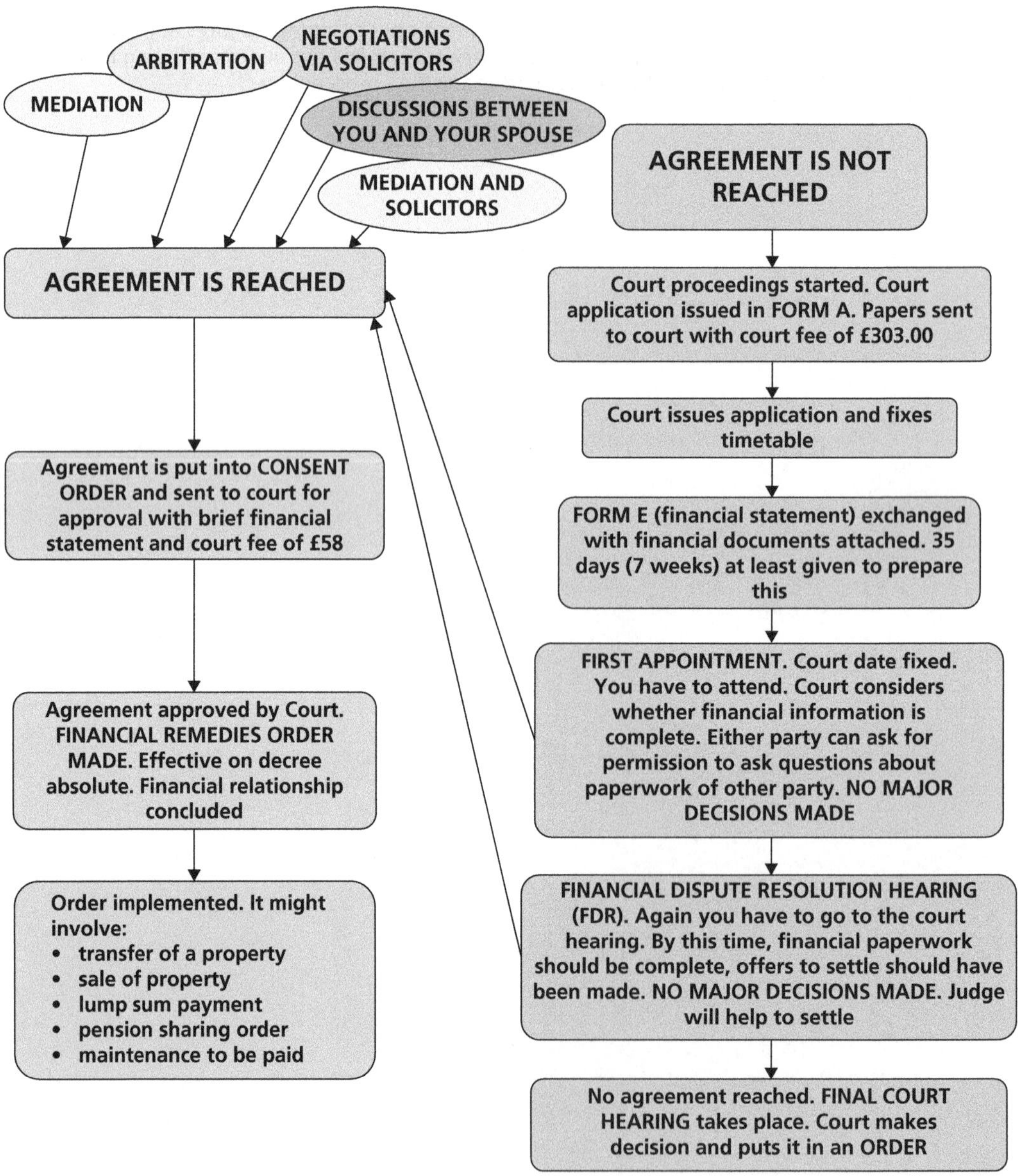


**Figure 1A:** Financial remedies

# Annex 1C

## Divorce and how it works

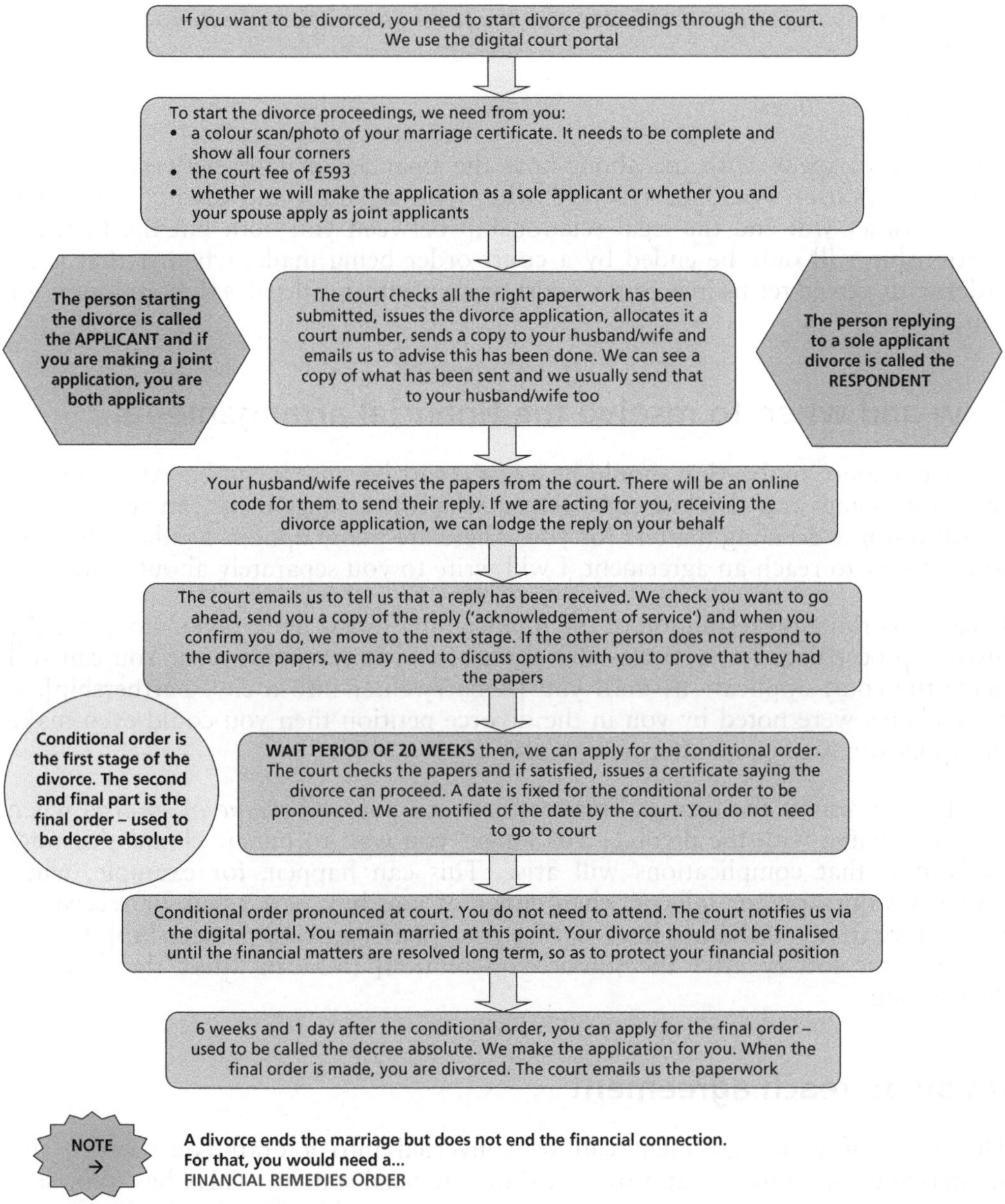


**Figure 1B:** Divorce and how it works

# Annex 1D

## Letter to client explaining applications that can be made for financial remedy

[*You may wish to convert this letter into the form of a leaflet or note to give to your client.*]

Dear [*name of client*]

You came to speak with me about how the financial matters between you and [*name of spouse*] would be resolved when you separate and divorce. The final divorce order will end the legal relationship between you both but the financial relationship will only be ended by a court order being made, whether that is an order with agreed terms in it or the court or an arbitrator decides the resolution for you.

## How and when to resolve the financial arrangements

Making a court application should be a last resort because it can be expensive and time consuming. You also lose control over what the arrangements can be if a judge or arbitrator is deciding matters for you. There are many options available for you to use to try to reach an agreement. I will write to you separately about that.

Usually, working on resolution of the financial matters is undertaken alongside the divorce proceedings but you can also do it after you have divorced. You can still make the court applications until you [remarry/enter into a civil partnership]. If these claims were noted by you in the divorce petition then you could even make the applications to court after remarriage.

It is best to resolve the financial matters between you and [*name of spouse*] when you are dealing with the divorce. The longer you wait to pursue claims the more likely it is that complications will arise. This can happen, for example, when property values rise or fall, or when either of you buy new assets or receive an inheritance that you did not have during your [marriage/civil partnership]. Even if you win the lottery after the [divorce/dissolution] this can affect the financial distribution.

## If you do reach agreement

The terms of your agreement can be converted into a draft court order and submitted to the court for approval. A short financial statement also has to be sent with the draft order to give the court some background and financial information. This is needed because the court does not 'rubber stamp' any agreement you have reached. The court will look carefully at the terms that you have agreed to consider whether the terms you have reached are fair. The court has discretion to accept or reject the terms of settlement.

## What orders can be made

There are no absolute answers and the law gives a large element of discretion. There may be a number of 'right' solutions.

A first consideration would be to try to end the financial relationship if possible. A second consideration would be for any children under the age of 18 and their housing needs. Both parents will remain financially responsible for their children and no obligation in that respect can be stopped by orders made between the parties to the marriage.

The scope of the financial assets must be clarified first of all. Then there is a consideration of what are matrimonial assets built up during the course of the marriage and what are non-matrimonial assets. The most common example of a non-matrimonial asset would be an inheritance. For most cases, the assets are not large enough to meet both parties' needs so non-matrimonial assets usually have to be used.

There is then a consideration of entitlement to the assets built up during the marriage and a consideration of what each of your financial needs are covering housing, income and pension in basic areas.

There are some basic principles that apply in all cases, however, and these can be summarised in a basic form as follows:

1. If you have children, one of the first concerns will be about housing for the children. It is not the overriding or only concern but it can be important.
2. If possible, the aim is to achieve a final settlement without continuing obligations towards each other so that you can move on with your lives. In a case with limited money, it can mean looking at meeting the needs of the parent with care of a child.
3. It is about fairness, so that you each take an equal drop in lifestyle and the presumption for the starting point for sharing assets is that you have equal shares. There are some factors that can change this but this depends on your circumstances.
4. Consideration is given to what you earn or could earn. This might mean you would be expected to get a job if you do not have one or re-train to be suitable for a different job if you cannot get work in your preferred area of employment.
5. All assets are considered but some can be treated differently to others, such as inheritances or money you had and kept separate before you married. The family home is always treated as a family asset. It does not matter in whose name the asset is held but this does not mean that it has to be divided equally. Assets accrued during the course of the marriage are all put into the 'pot' available for sharing.
6. Health, age and disability can sometimes affect a settlement.
7. Child maintenance is not dealt with by the court. If you can't reach agreement, you need to apply to the Child Maintenance Service (CMS) for them to assess child maintenance. If you do reach agreement, it can be recorded in an order but you are only bound by it for one year and then after that either one of you can make an application to the CMS for a child maintenance calculation. The part of the order dealing with child maintenance is then brought to an end. If you are very wealthy and earn more than £156,000 gross per annum, the court can order top-up child maintenance.

8. Pensions are relevant, whether state, private or employer pensions. Pensions can be very valuable. They are not the same as money in the bank, however, and cannot be drawn upon until you reach at least the age of 55.

The *types of orders* that can be made are:

1. Payments from one spouse to another (periodical payments orders, which are a type of income order – NOT the same as child maintenance).
2. Capital orders – lump sums, transfers of shares, transfers of ISAs.
3. Property transfer orders – transfer of the property from one spouse to the other.
4. Property sale orders – an order for the property to be sold.
5. Pension orders.

## *Income orders*

The court has the power to make various income orders for either your benefit, or [*name of spouse*]'s benefit. Payments can also be made to one of you for the benefit of the children or to the children direct – but see below about child maintenance.

Payments that are made between you and [*name of spouse*] are known as 'periodical payments' orders. One of you could be made to pay the other a regular monthly sum of money for a specified period of time or until the occurrence of a specific event.

The circumstances and length of the order depend very much upon the ages of any children, the amount that each of you can be expected to earn and the overall circumstances of the case. An order will be made if one party needs money (e.g. to pay bills and housing costs) and the other party has surplus income (after bills and housing costs have been paid) from which 'periodical payments' can be made.

The court cannot make an order for one party to pay the other periodical payments once the receiving party remarries. It is mandatory that periodical payments end upon remarriage.

## *Child maintenance*

Child maintenance is usually dealt with by agreement or as assessed by the CMS. The court cannot deal with child maintenance unless the parent who does not live with the child earns more than £156,000 gross per annum. The court can order 'top up' maintenance in addition to regular child maintenance for high earners (see below).

## *Capital orders*

The court can make lump sum orders for either you or [*name of spouse*] to pay the other a sum of money. This could be a one-off payment or a series of payments over a period of time. The structure of the payment will depend on the circumstances of the case.

The payment can be ordered to be made on a specified date or at the same time as the transfer or sale of a property

### *Property claims*

It is possible for you to make a claim against any property that you own jointly with [*name of spouse*] or that [*name of spouse*] owns solely in [his/her] name. A claim against property can be a claim against land, residential property or even commercial property owned by [*name of spouse*].

The court can make an order to sell or transfer property either in England and Wales or abroad, or to change the terms on which it is owned and when any equity can be realised.

[Any property owned by a trust or a limited company is beyond the direct reach of the court. As such the court cannot make orders to sell or transfer such property.]

The court can also make orders transferring shares, life policies, contents of your property or collector's items.

### *Financial support now*

In some circumstances, the court can make an urgent order for one party to pay the other party maintenance while the proceedings for divorce/civil partnership are ongoing. As an interim measure, maintenance is usually paid at a lower rate than it might be in the long term. Interim maintenance is meant to cover the basic essentials, excluding long-term and capital expenses.

As set out above, the court will only make such an order in circumstances where the paying party has sufficient surplus income from which to pay maintenance and the receiving party has a shortfall of income and cannot pay their bills and other outgoings.

### *Legal services payment orders*

It is possible to make an application to the court for [*name of spouse*] to pay your legal costs upfront if you are unable to find a way to pay for these costs yourself. This can be an expensive application to make and we should discuss this option, together with other funding options if you are unable to pay for your legal costs by using your own resources.

### *Maintenance orders for children*

The CMS generally deals with maintenance for children. The CMS website contains a wealth of information and I recommend that you look at it. There is an online calculator at **www.gov.uk/calculate-your-child-maintenance** that will help you and [*name of spouse*] to calculate the minimum sum of maintenance that should be paid.

There are limited circumstances in which the court will make an order for payments specifically for children.

Most commonly this will happen where you and [*name of spouse*] agree a sum of money that one of you will pay to the other for the benefit of the child(ren). This type of order by agreement is only binding upon both parties for the period of 12 months from the date of the order. After that period of time, either party can go to the CMS and make an application for a CMS calculation.

The court also has the ability to make orders in respect of children in the following additional circumstances:

1. where the child(ren) suffer(s) from a disability;
2. where the child(ren) [is/are] in full-time education or training;
3. where the paying parent has been assessed to pay the maximum sum by the CMS, the court has the jurisdiction to make a 'top up' order;
4. where either parent or the child resides overseas.

It is possible that the maintenance can extend beyond a child's 18th birthday and beyond the time a child is at university, in certain circumstances. It is important to note that the financial obligations you each have for your children cannot be terminated, unlike the financial obligations you and your spouse/civil partner may have towards each other.

### *Pension orders*

The court can make the following types of pension order:

1. pension attachment;
2. pension sharing.

[Where pensions are being administered by the Pension Protection Fund the court can make the above orders against the Pension Protection Fund rather than the trustees of the pension. These are known as compensation orders.]

Pension orders are fairly complex and it may be that an expert's report is required in order to help you to decide how to structure a settlement. I will advise you when we need an expert's report. Please do not commission an expert's report yourself as this is usually done in a specific way to ensure that it can be used in court proceedings.

As soon as I know more about the pensions in your case I will advise you further.

### *Costs orders*

It is very rare in family finance proceedings for the court to make a costs order. The general rule that the court will follow is that each party will pay their own legal costs.

In rare circumstances, the court will make a costs order against your [spouse/civil partner].

The court will usually do so in the following circumstances:

1. where one party refuses to use or consider non-court dispute resolution to try to resolve matters outside of court proceedings;
2. where one party has failed to comply with orders of the court, rules or practice directions;
3. where one party has pursued their case unreasonably;
4. where a party has defended their case unreasonably;
5. where one party made a reasonable open offer that should have been accepted but the other party did not accept it and thereby incurred further costs.

The court will only make orders where it is just and reasonable in all of the circumstances to do so and where it would not destabilise the final division of assets to make a costs order.

From my experience, costs orders are made in less than 1% of cases. You should therefore be ready to fund your own litigation proceedings. There is little chance for the recovery of your legal costs unless [*name of spouse*] does something that the court considers sufficiently serious to justify departing from the general rule. This is because each of you is paying your costs out of family money.

I hope you understand the orders that the court is able to make. If you have any questions or queries please do not hesitate to contact me.

Yours sincerely

# Annex 1E

## Letter/paragraphs explaining pension options

I note that your spouse has a pension(s) that you might eventually share in some way. Pensions are a complex subject area and you might not be clear how to proceed in respect of this asset.

Pensions are specialist, tax efficient investment vehicles that are designed to produce an income when you retire. They are not the same as an ISA or cash in the bank. They can only be accessed after age 55 (at present). For divorce purposes, valuations of the pensions are provided by the pension administrators but these are sometimes a poor reflection of the benefits that the scheme will provide. Some schemes have valuable benefits that would be lost on transfer.

I would strongly recommend that you take independent financial advice from an adviser who is experienced in pensions and divorce matters at an early stage in respect of [*name of spouse*]'s pension(s) and the overall financial settlement. A number of financial advisers are accredited through an organisation called Resolution and any one of them will be able to assist you. If you do not have a financial adviser, I can recommend the following independent financial advisers with whom I have worked in the past and who understand the importance of pensions within the divorce process.

1.
2.
3.

There are a number of choices that you will eventually need to make about the pension(s). Although I will give you legal advice, I cannot provide you with financial advice (as this would be an offence under the Financial Services and Markets Act 2000) so you should also take independent financial advice. The financial adviser will be able to speak to you about cash planning through your retirement.

[*Name of spouse*] has a pension(s) and in respect of each pension you can take a share of the pension, attach it or offset your interest in the pension against other assets.

Pensions are complex assets and the value of a pension fund and the income it produces on retirement are two distinct matters.

## Pension sharing

The court can make an order that [*name of spouse*]'s pension(s) are shared with you. In simple terms, this means part of the pension of [other party] is taken and put into a pension in your name, ready for when you retire. This is called your 'pension credit'.

You can either agree between you what percentage of the pension you will share, or the court will decide whether to make a pension sharing order and then the amount.

In general, the person with the larger pension(s) will share some of their pension(s) with the person who has less by way of pension benefits.

Normally, all pensions including the state pension are taken into account when calculating an appropriate percentage share. Sometimes the court can decide to exclude pensions that were built up before the date of the marriage. The court has the discretion to do this and may use it in appropriate cases.

If there is a mix of types of pensions or the pensions are worth more than £100,000 in total, it is likely that a report from a pension expert will be needed to advise how pensions should be shared. The aim is either to consider equalisation of the income from a pension in retirement or to equalise the capital value.

What happens to your pension credit depends on the pensions and the terms of the schemes. In some cases, the pension trustees will allow you to become a separate member of the same scheme as your ex-spouse. In others, they may insist on an external transfer of your pension share to a personal pension of your choice. For some schemes, you are not allowed to take the pension credit to another pension. As the choices can be complex, independent financial advice should be sought to establish which route is the best for you.

Only an independent financial adviser will be able to give you advice about what to do with your pension share once you get it. My role is to ensure that you get a fair share of assets, and once I have done that the financial adviser will tell you where to invest your pension.

Once pension sharing has been put into effect by the trustees of [*name of spouse*]'s pension, you will have your own pension fund.

Once you receive a share of [*name of spouse*]'s pension, this becomes your pension. It can't be taken away from you and it can't be varied. If [*name of spouse*] dies 28 days or more after you get a pension sharing order, your entitlement to get this pension is not affected by [his/her] death. You decide when you want to take your pension, subject to the rules of the pension scheme.

There are often fees to be paid to the pension administrators to implement a pension sharing order. The court would usually expect those fees to be shared equally between you both.

## Pension attachment

This is another option for taking an interest in [*name of spouse*]'s pension. This option is rarely used these days as it does not create a 'clean break', which many individuals prefer. If you choose pension attachment you become entitled to a proportion of your ex-partner's pension but have no influence over when or how your ex-partner takes benefits.

This can cause problems if [*name of spouse*] decides not to take the income from this pension until the age of 75, for example. The court has no power to order [*name of spouse*] to retire on a certain date or at a specific age. If [*name of spouse*] dies, then your entitlement to [his/her] pension income will stop. If you remarry, you will lose your pension income under the terms of this order.

Although the court will set out your entitlement to [*name of spouse*]'s pension in an order, this will always be subject to the possibility that [*name of spouse*] will apply for a variation of the order in the future. This means that the pension attachment order is not fixed but is subject to change.

After a pension attachment order has been made, [*name of spouse*] could stop making any contribution to this pension. You are not permitted to make a contribution to the pension as it remains in [*name of spouse*]'s name. This means that the pension may not increase in value at all between now and when [*name of spouse*] takes the pension income. You can of course start a pension in your sole name which is a matter you should discuss with your financial adviser.

Overall, most people find that pension attachment offers little certainty and so would not choose this option, although in rare cases there are valid reasons for considering it.

## Pension offsetting

This is a way to take other assets instead of touching [*name of spouse*]'s pension(s). The difficulty is that there is no widely accepted way of calculating what is a fair sum to take instead of sharing the pension. The higher courts have stated that £1 in a pension fund is not worth £1 in savings, but we do not know any more than that.

The pension expert can be asked to calculate how much your share in [*name of spouse*]'s pension should be worth as an offsetting figure. This can be a useful aid to settlement or to a judge when deciding how the assets should be shared between you.

Pensions are complex so please do ask questions if you need to.

[*Add in for client link to Advicenow booklet produced for a litigant in person.*]

# Annex 1F

## Letter to client explaining the different processes that can be used to resolve a financial remedy matter

Dear [*name of client*]

Many thanks for coming to see me with regard to your situation. I write to outline a number of dispute resolution processes that are available to you. These processes are voluntary and would require [*name of spouse*] to agree before you can proceed to use any of them.

As you know, I am a [Resolution member/Resolution accredited specialist/Member of the Family Law Accreditation at the Law Society/Member of the Family Law Advanced Accreditation at the Law Society]. This means that I am bound by the [Resolution code of conduct] as well as the [Law Society's Family Law Protocol]. I am therefore committed to ensuring that I minimise any potential conflict within your relationship breakdown, as much as I am able to do so.

Many people think that they should have their 'day in court', which will lead to a final resolution of the dispute. In reality, this is not how modern disputes are usually resolved. The vast majority of people are able to reach a negotiated settlement without ever needing to issue a court application.

With that in mind I have outlined below various low-conflict options that you may choose to take advantage of to try to resolve any children or financial matters between you and [*name of spouse*]. There are many financial and other advantages that support using one or more of the options below.

## Mediation

Mediation is a dispute resolution process that works very well for many couples. Many people confuse the process of mediation with that of reconciliation. The purpose of mediation is to support you to make decisions when you decide that your relationship has ended. Reconciliation is the process that you would go through if you want to get back together with [*name of spouse*].

The mediator is a neutral person who can help you and [*name of spouse*] to make decisions. I am happy to recommend to you a mediator who will be able to assist you through any conflict areas. Mediation is one of the most cost-effective and time-effective ways to resolve disputes. Mediators tend to have an average of three to six meetings with a couple to help you to resolve both children and financial matters.

Legal aid is still available to help fund the process of mediation and it may be that this is available to either you or [*name of spouse*], if you qualify. If you are mediating in respect of the arrangements for your children, you would be eligible for a voucher worth £500 under the government scheme available for all. If this is not an option, the precise cost is difficult to estimate, but I would expect the cost to be between £XX and £XX.

Each mediator charges a different hourly rate and so you will need to find out the specific costs from the mediator when you are referred. I would recommend that you look at the video available at **www.gov.uk/government/publications/family-mediation**, as it will give you a good idea what mediation is and what mediators do.

If you are not able to reach an agreement during the mediation process, an outcome cannot be imposed on you. Additionally, anything that is said within mediation cannot be referred to in later court proceedings.

## Collaborative law

Collaborative law is a process whereby both parties engage solicitors who are specialists and who are trained in the collaborative law process.

This can be a low-conflict process and result in agreed settlements much more quickly than via litigation. The parties and their solicitors commit to the process of negotiation to avoid litigation. The solicitor's commitment is such that if the process does not result in an agreement, the solicitor will not be able to represent you in the litigation process. [I am trained in the collaborative law process] *or* [I am happy to refer you to a collaboratively trained solicitor] *or* [*Name of solicitor*] in our practice is collaboratively trained].

The cost of the collaborative law process is variable, as this usually depends on the hourly rate of each solicitor involved. It is likely to cost in the region of £XX–£XX plus VAT.

If you are not able to reach an agreement during the collaborative law process, an outcome cannot be imposed on you.

## Arbitration

Arbitration more closely resembles the court process because the arbitrator can make a decision if you and [*name of spouse*] do not reach an agreement first. The arbitrator can deal with most financial cases and in your case there does not seem to be any reason why you should not be able to use arbitration. If you are interested in using this process, please have a look at the leaflet prepared by the Institute of Family Arbitrators, available at **https://ifla.org.uk/divi/wp-content/uploads/Public.pdf**.

If the arbitration process is used, an independent arbitrator will be chosen by you and [*name of spouse*]. The arbitrator will ensure that the evidence is collected and that each party has the opportunity to 'have their say'. The arbitrator then uses the information to make a decision about the division of assets, income, pensions and property between the parties. The decision of an arbitrator is called the arbitration 'award'.

## Consent order

In each of the above processes, if a settlement is reached, a draft consent order will need to be prepared and sent to the Family Court. A judge has the power to accept or reject the terms of settlement that you reach between you at mediation or using the collaborative process.

If the consent order reflects the terms of an arbitrator's award it will not be rejected unless there are exceptional reasons to do so.

To many people it seems strange that a judge can refuse to accept the terms of an agreement that you have both reached between you. If the terms of the agreement are fair, the judge won't interfere with the terms of the settlement. Sometimes the judge wants to know more about the settlement between the parties and asks questions before the terms of the draft order are approved.

On other occasions the judge will have some concerns about the way the document is drafted, and this will result in the order being re-drafted.

All judges have an absolute right to raise any questions that they want to.

Very rarely, the judge will reject the terms of the settlement if they are deemed to be too favourable to one party. In this situation we will need to sit down and discuss the options going forward in your case.

Overall, the costs for drafting a consent order will be between £XX plus VAT and £XX plus VAT, depending on how complicated the order is and whether the judge raises questions about the terms. There is also a court fee to pay for asking the court to approve an order.

Please let me know if you would like any more information about any of the above processes so that you can decide how to progress matters forward.

Yours sincerely

# Annex 1G

### Letter to client regarding change of circumstances

Dear [*name of client*]

Many thanks for your instructions in this matter. I write to advise you that while I have given you my initial views on the settlement options, it is possible that these views might change.

## Possible future changes of advice

I appreciate that this is a difficult time for you and your family and that you would like to make decisions based on the best advice. Unfortunately, the progress of litigation can be quite slow and this means that as your assets change and your personal circumstances change my advice may also need to change.

## Legal costs

As a general rule of thumb, both parties will spend roughly equal sums on legal costs and these funds will therefore not be available to distribute. I refer you back to my initial estimate of costs in this matter. It can take 12 months or more to reach a final financial order, either by agreement or by order of the court. The money and property available to distribute at the end of the case may be quite different from that available at the beginning of the case.

## The influence of higher courts

You should also be aware that the courts can sometimes change their attitudes towards certain outcomes. This can happen when a case is resolved by the Supreme Court or the Court of Appeal and this impacts on similar cases ongoing in the Family Court across the country. I will try to ensure that you are made aware of any cases similar to yours that might be dealt with in the higher courts. To the best of my knowledge, there are no such cases at the moment. As family law specialists, we do everything we can to ensure that we keep you informed of such changes as and when they occur. Please rest assured that these changes happen infrequently.

## Evidence changes

As time goes on in the litigation process, we will collect evidence from you and your spouse to send to court. Occasionally, my advice will change as a result of evidence produced which may impact on the case as I thought it was when I initially gave you advice.

## Financial division

As I have already explained to you, there is no formula that guides the distribution of assets in divorce proceedings. This means that I can only advise you by using my knowledge of the way in which the Family Court in [*location*] deals with these matters in cases similar to yours.

I will do the best that I can to minimise any unnecessary changes of advice. You can help me by ensuring that I receive your evidence when I ask you to provide it to me. You should also inform me of any change in circumstances as soon as it happens.

Yours sincerely

# Annex 1H

### Letter to petitioner client regarding when to apply for the final divorce order

Dear [*name of client*]

The conditional divorce order was made on [*date*] and I enclose a copy for you. This is the first part of your divorce and you still remain married. Through this order being made, the jurisdiction of the court is open to make or approve financial orders.

## When you can apply for the final divorce order

[*Sole application*] As you are the applicant in the divorce, you are entitled to apply for the final divorce order six weeks and one day after the date of the conditional divorce order. The earliest date that you can apply is [*date*].

## Delay the application for final divorce order

We usually recommend that you do not apply for the final divorce order until the financial matters have been resolved by way of a final financial remedy order. This is very important and there are very good reasons not to make the application.

If your spouse has a pension, you will currently benefit from a widow's/widower's pension in the event that your spouse dies before the final divorce order is pronounced.

When the final divorce order is pronounced, you will no longer be married to each other and you will not benefit from any widow's/widower's pension if your spouse dies before we get a final financial order. It is possible that you will receive a pension sharing order as part of the overall financial settlement. It is sensible to wait for the final financial order to be made before you apply for the final divorce order, so that your right to your spouse's death benefit is protected. We may also advise you to wait for a further period after a financial order is made that includes a pension sharing order.

You might think that it is in your interests to apply for the final divorce order at the first opportunity. If you would prefer to apply as soon as you can, we should discuss this.

## When can [*name of spouse*] apply for the final divorce order?

Eventually, [*name of spouse*] can apply for the final divorce order in their own right. The first date that [he/she] may do so is 3 months after the first date that you can apply. I calculate that [*name of spouse*] will be able to apply for the final divorce order on [*date*].

## Can we stop [*name of spouse*] from applying for the final divorce order?

We may be able to prevent [*name of spouse*] from applying for the final divorce order by asking them to give us an undertaking not to apply for the final divorce order until the final financial order is made. An undertaking is a solemn promise not to do something; however, [*name of spouse*] is not obliged to give us that promise.

If [*name of spouse*] does not give that promise, you should be aware that recent case law suggests that [*name of spouse*] will be able to obtain the final divorce order unless there are exceptional circumstances that prevent it from being granted. Your case does not exhibit the necessary exceptional circumstances. In my view, we would be unlikely to persuade a court to prevent your spouse from obtaining the final divorce order. We can discuss this possibility at the point at which you can apply for the final divorce order as we should know more about the financial settlement by then.

[***To be used in cases where there is a home rights notice***: As your spouse owns the former matrimonial home in [his/her] sole name we have registered your right to occupy the property. If you apply for the final divorce order to be granted then you will no longer be married to each other and your right to occupy the property will terminate. Your spouse will be able to cancel the home rights notice by submitting the final divorce order to the Land Registry. We may be able to make an application to extend your right to occupy the property.]

## Wills

You should also be aware that while you remain married your existing Wills continue to take effect against each other. Once the final divorce order is pronounced you will both need to make new Wills.

Should you wish to discuss this any further please do not hesitate to contact me.

Yours sincerely

## Annex 1I

### Letter to client to sever joint tenancy

Dear [*name of client*]

I am writing to you further to our meeting as I have now obtained the necessary information from the Land Registry in respect of your property.

It is clear to me now that you and [*name of co-owner*] own the property at [*address(es) of property*] as Joint Tenants. This means that you own the property as a whole between you and that in the event either of you dies, the other will automatically own the whole property. This is known as the right of survivorship.

It is possible to change the way that you own the property by doing what is known as 'severing the joint tenancy'. This is done by preparing a legal document and sending it to [*name of spouse*]. If you want to do this, then you and [*name of spouse*] will still be joint owners but you will own the property as Tenants in Common. This will mean that you will each own 50% of the property and you will each be able to leave your share by Will to whoever you wish.

It is not possible to sever the tenancy in unequal shares. Choosing to sever the tenancy now will not jeopardise your claim in financial proceedings to a greater share of the equity in this property. It will not limit the way in which the Court can deal with the property in the financial case.

This is an interim measure designed to allow you flexibility to leave your share of the property on death to whoever you choose.

It is your choice whether you decide to sever the tenancy or not. You should be aware that once the tenancy is severed, [*name of spouse*]'s share will not pass to you automatically in the event of their death.

Please can you let me know in writing whether you wish to sever the joint tenancy. You can do this by signing the enclosed copy of this letter and sending it to me. I will then prepare the necessary paperwork to send to [*name of co-owner*].

It is vital that you make a Will at the same time as severing the joint tenancy. This is so that you leave your share to your chosen beneficiaries.

If you choose to go ahead, then once the tenancy has been severed I will register this change at the Land Registry.

Yours sincerely

[***Insert signature clause on a duplicate copy of the letter***]

I confirm that I do/not want you to go ahead and sever the tenancy for the above property.

# Annex 1J

## Letter to client to explain home rights charge or restrictions

Dear [*name of client*]

I am writing to you further to our meeting as I have now obtained the necessary information from the Land Registry in respect of the property(ies) discussed in our last meeting.

It is clear to me now that [*name of spouse*] owns the family home at [*address of property*] in [his/her] sole name. As this property was [the family home/intended to be used as the family home] you are entitled to register your right to occupy the property. I can complete the form and send it to the Land Registry. When I do this the Land Registry will add a notice to the register. This means that for the duration of your marriage you are legally entitled to occupy the property. This right does not automatically give you any financial interest in the property, which could be established though the court proceedings.

Once the final divorce order in the divorce/dissolution proceedings is pronounced you will lose your right to occupy the property. It is possible but rare for your right of occupation to be terminated by a court order.

I will complete the Land Registry form and lodge it with the Land Registry as soon as you authorise me to do so. You should be aware that [*name of spouse*] will be notified by the Land Registry that you have made this application. If you think that this is going to cause problems for you at home then we should discuss this matter before I send the form.

[***If the other party owns more than one property in their sole name, use this paragraph*** – I have also obtained information that shows your spouse owns the following properties in [his/her] sole name:

1.
2.
3.

If possible we should register a restriction at the Land Registry against each of the above properties. This should ensure that if your spouse attempts to sell or charge these properties, any prospective buyer or lender is made aware that you have an interest in these properties. It doesn't necessarily prevent your spouse from selling the property, but you should be notified of any prospective sale and then we could make any necessary applications to the court to prevent a sale from completing.]

We can at the same time register a restriction against the family home so that your financial interest is protected as well as your right to occupy the property.

I look forward to hearing from you about this matter. If it is easier for you to do so please sign the bottom of this letter to indicate how you wish to proceed.

Yours sincerely

I [*name of client*] of [*address*] confirm that I have read your letter above and that I [would like/do not want] you to proceed to register a home rights notice against the property at [*address*].

[Additionally I would like you to register a restriction against the properties at:

1.
2.
3. ]

I understand that [*name of spouse*] will receive notification from the Land Registry that I have made these applications.

.....................................................

Signed by [*name of client*]

# Annex 1K

### Child maintenance scheme[1]

A new child maintenance scheme based on **gross** income was introduced by the government in December 2012. All cases dealt with under the old scheme based on **net** income were transferred to the new scheme by 31 December 2017.

## Charges to use the CMS (Child Maintenance Service, which has taken over from the Child Support Agency (CSA))

The CMS expects parents to make the payment arrangements between themselves – 'Direct Pay'. If the CMS collects the payments because payment is not being made or a payment is missed ('Collect & Pay'), the paying parent has to pay an additional 20% of the assessed fee to the CMS in charges. The receiving parent has to pay 4% to the CMS in charges.

## The current gross income scheme

1. Calculate gross income. This is the total of all of the non-resident parent's income from employment, self-employment and pensions. It is possible to deduct pension contributions from the gross income figure but there are anti-avoidance provisions to prevent high pension payments being made to divert income.
2. Apply rates:

| Number of children | % of gross weekly income up to £800 pw | % applied to gross income between £801 and £3,000 |
|---|---|---|
| 1 | 12% | 9% |
| 2 | 16% | 12% |
| 3 or more | 19% | 15% |

3. Make a deduction for other children living in the non-resident parent's household (for example, children of a new partner or step-children) at the following rates:
   (a) 11% for one child;
   (b) 14% for two children; and
   (c) 16% for three or more children.
4. Apply any reduction for shared care:
   (a) 1/7th for 52–103 nights.
   (b) 2/7th for 104–155 nights
   (c) 3/7th for 156–174 nights.
   (d) ½ for 175 or more nights.

1. Extracted to give to clients.

Note that if there is truly equal shared care, no child maintenance is payable via the CMS. However, if one parent receives child benefit then there is a presumption that that parent is providing care for the child and should receive child maintenance. Applications can be made to court for child maintenance where the CMS does not deal with child maintenance.

## Income figures used

The figures used are 'historical' i.e. taken from your last P60 or last completed tax return. The assessment is reviewed annually. If during the course of the year, your income situation changes by 25% or more, you can ask to be assessed on your current income basis rather than the historical income basis. For example:

- You earned £40,000 and have been made redundant. Your earnings are now zero.
- You were earning £50,000 but you moved to another role and took a pay cut to £37,500.

## Applying for a downwards variation

A parent paying child maintenance can apply for a reduction for the following reasons:

1. Cost of maintaining contact with the child – if you have to travel a long way.
2. Costs of a long-term illness or disability.
3. Previous debts incurred before the couple separated.
4. Boarding school fees paid for the child.
5. Costs of repaying a mortgage on the home of the person with care of the child (but not if the mortgage is in your name).

All of these have different criteria and we can advise further if any of these apply to you.

## Applying for an upwards variation

The person receiving the maintenance can apply for an upward variation on the basis of:

1. Unearned income, e.g. income/interest from investments or rent from a property.
2. Diverted income, e.g. where you have given/put your income elsewhere.
3. Income from high value assets worth more than £31,250.

If the non-resident parent has unearned income of at least £2,500 from property (rent), savings, investments or certain other sources then it is possible to apply for a variation to the maintenance assessment. The extent of the non-resident parent's income from these sources is determined on the basis of information provided to HMRC.

Diversion of income is designed to capture the situation where the non-resident parent can control the amount of income that he or she receives or the situation in which the non-resident parent pays income to another person or elsewhere to reduce his or her own income.

The rules are complex and there is no obligation to report changes in this type of income.

If the non-resident parent's gross income is assessed at more than £156,000 per annum, it is possible to apply to the court for additional child maintenance on top of maintenance assessed by the CMS.

# Annex 1L

## Interim maintenance (maintenance pending suit)

## What?

There are different types of maintenance. Child maintenance – usually assessed by the Child Maintenance Service – is always payable when there are children involved. Spousal maintenance – an income payment from one spouse to another – is not always payable, and is rarely payable for the vast majority of cases.

Spousal maintenance could be payable until the death of the person receiving it (rarely), or for a period of time to allow one party to adjust, or not at all. It depends on the financial circumstances of each family and, often, balancing the needs of each.

### *Interim maintenance – maintenance pending suit*

This type of maintenance is payable as an 'interim' measure until the long-term arrangements are made. It is often referred to as interim maintenance, although the correct name is maintenance pending suit. It can only be paid from the date of a divorce application – so you have to start divorce proceedings – however an application for a financial order has to be made at the same time. In other words, although you are applying for 'interim' income payments, you are making an application for the long-term arrangements to be resolved at the same time.

## How much?

Careful consideration should be given to the proportionality of an application for maintenance pending suit. In cases where the assets are limited, the costs of such an application may outweigh the benefits. Efforts should be made to agree interim provision before the issue of an application. Maintenance pending suit has been described as 'designed to deal with short term cash flow problems', and it is risky making an application to the court because if the application is unsuccessful, the court can order costs against the unsuccessful party. These types of applications are expensive in terms of legal costs and for that reason, are rarely made, especially where assets are limited/modest and the focus should be on resolving matters overall in the long term.

It is only income payments that are dealt with and not lump sum payments.

The criteria are about 'reasonableness', and that is why it can be risky. One person's view of reasonable is not necessarily the same as the court's view – or each judge's view.

Detailed budgets of critical/essential need must be produced and these are scrutinised carefully by the court. The court can reduce the budget or cut out an expense if it thinks it is unreasonable. Generally, holidays, clothing and savings are excluded. It is about what you are actually paying out for and need. For example, if you are paying your car insurance monthly, that is included. If you have paid your car insurance for the year in advance, there will not be an allowance for you saving each month for the next year's premium. That will fall due when it falls due.

*If you need help with this topic, speak to us.*

# Annex 1M

## Guidance to client on self-help

## Their paperwork is in the house that we are still having to share so I should get copies of it for myself, right?

No. There can be very serious consequences to acting in this way. I do not advise that you do this at all.

Confidential information includes communications concerned with an individual's private life including personal finances, personal business dealings and possibly other business dealings. The European Convention on Human Rights (ECHR) Article 8 confers a right to respect for privacy and specifically mentions correspondence.

## What consequences?

- A spouse whose confidential information has been taken is entitled to seek relief such as an injunction preventing the further examination or use of the information, an order for the return of the documents, and an order for the return or destruction of any copies.
- Intercepting mail addressed to another may be a criminal offence under the Postal Services Act 2000, s.84 (see also the Investigatory Powers Act 2016).
- Telephone tapping of a public telephone may be a criminal offence (see Investigatory Powers Act 2016) and is likely also to be an actionable breach of confidence and/or breach of privacy under the Human Rights Act 1998. Although it is not a criminal offence under the Investigatory Powers Act 2016 for someone to record their private telephone line (if they have the right to control the operation or use of the system), there may be issues arising under the Human Rights Act 1998.
- Misuse of electronic and other data. The Computer Misuse Act 1990 makes it an offence to have unauthorised access to computer material and to modify computer material without authority. The consequences may be both criminal and civil, and the sanctions include potential imprisonment/fines. The Act predates the technology it now has to deal with, and it seems that the term 'computer' now has a meaning that is wider than could possibly have been anticipated when the legislation was enacted. It is safest to assume that computer material may include any information held on any electronic device with capacity for memory storage/access including, for example, home or business computers/servers/networks, laptops, external hard drives, memory sticks/disks/CDs, tablets, mobile phones and information contained within any private email account or private social network.
- The data protection legislation requires those who hold personal data to deal with it in accordance with principles and rules, and applies to private individuals and businesses. Higher standards apply to sensitive personal data. Sanctions for breach may include fines, criminal sanctions, and possible civil claims (for example, for breach of statutory duty). There have been a number of cases

where a data handler has misused the information (e.g. to track down an ex-wife or child).

- The Copyright Designs and Patents Act 1988 protects works, which may include text, pictures, data and software, created by individuals. If, for example, another individual copies the work of another, then damages may be awarded for any economic loss suffered as a result.

## What happens if they have done this?

1. If a party supplies improperly obtained documents to their solicitor, the solicitor must not read them and must immediately seek to obtain all of the improperly obtained documents from that party and return them to the other party's solicitor, including any copies.
2. The other party's solicitor must, in accordance with their duty to the court, read the documents and disclose those that are admissible and relevant in accordance with the duty of full and frank disclosure – if the solicitor is dis-instructed then the documents should be retained by them pending further directions from the court.
3. If the party from whom the documents have been improperly obtained does not have a solicitor then the documents should be retained, unread, in sealed files, by the solicitor acting for the party who improperly obtained them and directions sought from the court. The court's directions may include provision for the cost of an independent lawyer to be funded by the party who took the documents, in order to determine which documents are relevant and admissible.

If you think your documents have been taken, contact me. I will then contact your spouse or their solicitor and ask for the documents to be returned and any copies destroyed. I will then guide you through what needs to be disclosed.

Bear in mind, there is an absolute duty of full and frank disclosure in family financial proceedings. Anything less than full openness can cause an agreement to be set aside and all claims reopened.

# 2 Making a financial application

## 2.1 When to make the application

There should be serious consideration of aims and objectives before making an application to court. The aim should always be to settle matters for the client, whether that is pre or post an application being made. One of the main reasons for making an application is refusal to provide financial disclosure or poor financial disclosure. Another may be pace and lack of engagement. Keep an eye on the costs for your client. You should not be encouraging significant costs to be incurred pre-application without a material benefit to your client. At each stage, remind yourself again of the aims and objectives, and consider whether mediation, arbitration or simply picking up the telephone will help to resolve matters. Avoid just running through the routine of questions, schedules of deficiency and so on. You are a problem solver, enabling your client to make their decisions from an informed position. Remind yourself of the pre-application protocol for financial applications brought into force in May 2024 (see **Annex 3G**). Note that you are expected to send a copy of this to your client.

Ensure that you have discussed with your client the options around making an application, including updating your costs estimate. Make sure this is documented on your file and communicated to your client. Making an application should be a collaborative decision with your client so that expectations are understood and managed.

## 2.2 Using myHMCTS portals

For a solicitor representing a client, use of the HMCTS portal is mandatory. There are two portals; one for managing the solicitor organisation and one for managing case files. Each have different purposes and different login credentials.

To have access to the portals, your firm will need a Payment By Account (PBA) account with HMCTS. This is rather like a credit account. Your firm will be given a PBA number that is inserted on court forms to allow the court to make a debit to your account and collect the court fee. It is good business practice not to incur a court fee unless you are holding sufficient funds from your client to cover the outlay.

The court fees are taken from your firm's office account, either monthly or weekly depending on the set up with HMCTS.

Once the PBA account is set up, your firm may then register for myHMCTS to get access to the portals.

There are several walk-through guidance videos on YouTube and guidance notes on the gov.uk website. Functionality is added all the time to the portals, so make sure you keep up to date with additions.

The 16 digit case number system has replaced the old FamilyMan case numbering. Note that the case numbers for divorce and financial applications are different.

The system is simple to use, so explore it by clicking around.

## 2.3 Using myHMCTS Manage Organisation

Usually, only one or two senior personnel will use myHMCTS Manage Organisation. The purpose of the portal is to manage settings for the organisation as a whole and to allow cases to be allocated to the case handler. Within the myHMCTS system, the person handling these aspects is called the Case Access Administrator (CAA). Each case handler is called a 'user' and differing permissions can be set for each 'user'.

Any cases where you are acting for the respondent will come into your firm via this portal. The CAA should check the portal every day or at least every couple of days and then allocate the case to the appropriate case handler. Only then will the case appear in the list of cases for the case handler.

The login credentials for this portal are different to those for the case handler portal, so if you are the CAA and also a case handler, make sure you know both.

## 2.4 Using myHMCTS Manage Cases

You will find all of your active and closed cases in myHMCTS Manage Cases. Login requires your email address and password, and a numeric access code is then sent to your registered email address to complete the login. If you are experiencing 'double login' it will be because of a shortcut saved in your browser history. Clear your browser cache and start again.

The jurisdictional options within the portal are Family Divorce (which is divorce and financial remedy); Schedule 1 Children Act 1989 applications; probate; civil; and Family Private Law, which will be where the new private law children proceedings will sit when this is operative.

## 2.5 Applying for an order by consent

Within the portal, the option to select is 'Financial Remedy Consented'. You will be led through a series of screens to make your application. On paper, the form would have been a Form A, however, this is now incorporated within the screens of the system, so there is no need for a separate form to be uploaded.

You will be prompted to upload the conditional order (or final order if you have it). You will be prompted to upload the signed draft financial order, Form D81 and pension sharing annex. In respect of the format of these documents, they can all be PDF or Word. The pension sharing annex can be uploaded as a PDF document. If uploaded as an editable PDF or Word document, it is easier (and therefore quicker) for the court service to insert the date.

As part of lodging the documents, you are asked to select the correct area for the applicant. Remember it is the applicant's location and not your location that dictates where the case should be allocated, as it always was. If you are not sure of the area or local court, use the 'Find A Court or Tribunal' search function on the internet.

Only the applicant can apply for an order by consent. This option should not be used if either the case began on paper or a contested application was digitally issued and has been compromised.

## 2.6 Using the Form D81

The Form D81 has changed significantly over the last few years. It now presents a 'before and after' picture for the judge to refer to when considering whether to exercise their jurisdiction. Use the Form D81 fully and creatively. Your aim is to be helpful to a busy judge, explaining to them what has been agreed and why, in the context of application of the criteria of MCA 1973, s.25. Do not overlook the opportunity to do this.

You can add a breakdown in simpler terms for the judge as an Excel spreadsheet if you think it would be helpful. You can upload an Open Financial Statement from a successful mediation. Think – if you were the judge, what would you see (the draft order, Form D81 and pension annex) and so what else do you need to know to confidently exercise your jurisdiction?

You must also comply with the notice provisions set out in the Family Procedure Rules (FPR) 2010, SI 2010/2955, rules 9.13 and 32 in respect of notice to be given to third parties.

## 2.7 Applying for an order – contested procedure

The option in the myHMCTS portal is 'Contested Financial Remedy'. Again, the process for uploading the conditional order or final order is as for the consent journey. There is the additional option of uploading only the divorce application, recognising that a financial application may need to be made before the conditional order is granted. The process for selecting the court is the same.

From 29 April 2024, amendments to the Family Procedure Rules 2010 require your mediation information and assessment meeting (MIAM) certificate to be uploaded and, prior to the First Appointment, a statement in Form FM5 setting out your client's position in respect of non-court dispute resolution. This is required irrespective of when you issued your application. The case management powers of the court are such that proceedings can be adjourned or stayed, with a direction made for parties to attend a MIAM or comply with the filing requirement of Form FM5.

The types of application available mirror the paper Form A version. These are income, capital, property and pension orders. It is good practice to tick all, unless it is known there is no property.

In certain limited situations, the court will have the power to make financial remedy orders in respect of children. If those circumstances exist, the relevant boxes should be ticked.

If there is no agreement between the parties, the applicant needs to indicate how the court has jurisdiction to make an order.

It should be noted that if the applicant is hoping to obtain maintenance in addition to child support as assessed by the Child Maintenance Service (CMS), then the CMS must have produced a maximum assessment calculation before making the application to the court. It is not enough for the parties to agree that the CMS will produce a maximum assessment calculation to confer jurisdiction for child maintenance on the court.

Within the screens for the Form A, you are required to give details of the property, and if you have not obtained office copy entries for the properties in question, you should obtain them before lodging your application. You will need to provide the details for any properties and any mortgagees.

The system will allow you to apply for maintenance pending suit but this should only be selected if you are asking for an immediate hearing for maintenance pending suit to be addressed. The allocation certificate is also incorporated within the screens. (These are the selections about size of asset pool and complexity to dictate allocation between district judge and High Court level.)

You then wait for your Form A to be issued, together with the Form C and blank Form G. The court will serve the Form A and supporting documents upon the respondent. It is wise for you to also send a copy.

The portal should be viewed as the court file. The rules concerning service do not disappear and need to be complied with.

## 2.8 What to do when your Form A is issued

### *2.8.1 Service on third parties*

When you have received notification, you must comply with FPR 2010, rules 9.13 and 9.31 and thereafter, file your certificates of service (Form F6).

FPR 2010, rule 9.31 applies where a pension sharing order is applied for. The requirements for service are slightly different where an application is made for a pension attachment order. FPR 2010, rule 9.33 states that a copy of the sealed application must be served on the person responsible for the pension arrangement (PRPA) concerned. However, the applicant is also required to send details of an address for service of notices on the applicant and an address to which payments to the applicant should be sent. In addition, if the applicant's bank details are given, sufficient information should be provided to ensure that the payment can be made into the applicant's account.

It should be noted that the PRPA has 21 days from the date of service to ask that the person with pension rights provide information disclosed in the financial statement in relation to those rights or benefits.

It should therefore be noted that no other persons can be served with a copy of the sealed application without specific permission being sought from the court.

Those third parties who cannot automatically be served with a copy of the sealed application may need to be notified about the existence of the application. The solicitor must be careful that no confidential information is accidentally revealed in the initial letter. **Annex 2C** is a letter to a third party informing them that financial remedy proceedings have been issued by one of the parties to divorce proceedings, which can be adapted as appropriate.

A third party may be a joint owner of the property, may have an interest in the joint bank account or may allege that they have a beneficial interest in an asset owned by one of the parties to the divorce. The nature of a third party's interest should be specified in the precedent letter at para.2.

This letter should only be sent to a third party in the event that they purport to have a financial interest in assets that may be captured within the proceedings. An order from the court is required before the Form A can be served on the third party but advance notice by way of letter can be given. The third party may then take independent legal advice and decide that they want to be joined to the proceedings or that they want permission to intervene within the proceedings.

### *2.8.2 Communicating case plans with your client*

Your client needs to know what is likely to happen within the case. When the Form A is issued, you should send them a case plan letter, suggesting that they keep the letter and refer to it from time to time at different stages of the process. Remember, this is your day-to-day work but it is all new to your client.

### *2.8.3 Diary planning for you*

When you receive your Form C, you should begin diarising. You should diarise the due dates for documents to be filed and also include warning dates leading up to the due date so as to allow yourself plenty of time to prepare the papers, building in an allowance as you will need engagement from your client to achieve this.

It is suggested that you allow yourself a month to get the Form E ready, bearing in mind you need paperwork from your client. At the same time, you should be considering the Efficiency Statement. This requires the production of Form ES1 and Form ES2; production of property particulars suitable for your client and the other party; and an indication, jointly obtained if possible, of your client's mortgage capacity and that of their spouse if you are jointly obtaining it. The Efficiency Statement is available at **www.judiciary.uk/guidance-and-resources/notice-from-the-financial-remedies-court-4** and a note on the correct use of ES2 is available at **www.judiciary.uk/guidance-and-resources/notice-from-the-financial-remedies-court-2-2**.

It is recommended that you remind yourself of the wording of FPR 2010, Practice Direction 27A and the Efficiency Statement every time you need to prepare a bundle. Do not rely on your memory. Take care over your paperwork and ensure that the format complies with the practice directions. The first thing the court will see, even before you step into a court room, is your paperwork. Be proud of it and prepare it to be helpful to the court.

### *2.8.4 Tips for uploading documents*

There is a 'lock and key' facility for uploading documents. If you upload a document and denote it as confidential, only you and the judge will be able to see the document, and the document cannot be shared.

If you are uploading any other document, that document is not shared with the other party until you select the option to share the document, unless it is a document for FDR, which will be immediately visible to all in the FDR tab. This means that you can confidentially upload your Form E and bundle of documents knowing that the other party will not be able to access them until you share them. Note also that sharing documents in the portal is not service. You must also send them to the other party.

To make applications within the case (interlocutory applications) for an expert to be appointed, or for directions and so on, the application form D11 needs to be uploaded to the portal with the option for 'Create General Application' selected.

Orders for approval should be uploaded to 'Upload Draft Order' as a Word document so that the court can approve and issue them.

If the case is settled once the formal application has been made, the draft consent order, Form D81 and pension sharing annex(es) are also uploaded to 'Upload Draft Order'.

The court bundles that you prepare should be in PDF, paginated OCR format, compliant with the directions for the production of electronic bundles. The pagination should be consecutive not Bates numbering (i.e. do not use a system such as A1, A2 ..., B1, B2, etc.). The page number in the bundle must match the PDF page number (i.e. numbering must start with the first page of the pdf being numbered '1' and must be continuous afterwards). There is no limit to the size of the file that can be uploaded.

# Annex 2A

## Letter to mortgage company sending sealed Form A

Dear Sirs

Re: *[insert name of borrowers]*
*[insert name and address of property or land charged]*
*[insert mortgage account number if you know it]*

We represent [*name of client*] in [divorce] and matrimonial finance proceedings. Our client has made a financial application against the [property/land] detailed above.

We are required to notify you of our client's application because you have secured a mortgage against this [property/land]. We enclose a copy of our client's sealed application for your attention.

We should be grateful if you would acknowledge that you have received this letter so that we may confirm to the Court that we have complied with our obligation to notify you.

If you wish to intervene in these proceedings, you should contact the Family Court at [*insert name of court*] quoting case number [*insert case number*] and send a copy to me.

# Annex 2B

## Letter to pension trustees sending sealed Form A

Dear Sirs

**Re: *[insert name of pension member, National Insurance number, date of birth and pension plan number]***

We represent [*name of client*] in [divorce and] matrimonial finance proceedings. Our client has issued a financial application against the person with the pension detailed above. The financial applications made include those for a pension sharing order, a pension attachment order and compensation orders if these are applicable to this pension scheme.

We are required to notify you of our client's application, and as such we enclose a copy of our client's sealed application for your attention.

[***Additional paragraph to be included where an application has been made for a pension attachment order*:** The address where notices should be sent to the applicant is [*address*] and any payments ordered by the Court should be sent to the applicant at [*insert payment details*].]

We should be grateful if you would acknowledge that you have received this letter so that we may confirm to the Court that we have complied with our obligation to notify you.

# Annex 2C

## Letter to a third party advising them about financial remedy proceedings

Dear Sirs

Re: *[insert names of the parties to a divorce]*

We represent [*name of client*] in [divorce and] matrimonial finance proceedings. Our client has issued a financial application against [*name of spouse*].

We understand that you have an interest in the parties' financial affairs as [*explain in detail the third party's potential interest*]. Our client therefore puts you on notice that [he/she] has made a financial application in the Family Court at [*insert name of court*]. The proceedings have been issued under case reference [*insert case number*].

Should you wish to assert your right over [*insert details of potential third party rights that may be affected by a financial remedy order*] you should take immediate independent legal advice. You should let your legal adviser know that the [first/next] hearing in this matter is the [First Appointment/financial dispute resolution hearing/directions appointment] and you may wish to put forward your case about [*insert details of potential third party rights*] before that hearing takes place.

We are not able to give you any advice in respect of this matter, but would suggest that you see a specialist family law solicitor. If you do not have a family law solicitor, you can find one by using the Law Society 'find a solicitor' function at **www.lawsociety.org.uk**.

If you choose not to have a solicitor, you can contact us direct.

# Annex 2D

## Leaflet to client: what are legal services orders?

### What is a legal services order?

This is a court order where one spouse/civil partner is ordered to make a payment, either monthly or a lump sum, to the other party to enable them to pay for their solicitor. It is also called 'a legal services payment order'.

This type of order is available in proceedings for divorce/dissolution/(judicial) separation and in connected financial remedy proceedings.

The law states that the court may also make such an order in connection with proceedings for divorce, nullity of marriage or judicial separation. Slightly different rules apply to other proceedings.

### What are 'legal services'?

Legal services are defined as:

- advice on how the law applies in the particular circumstances;
- advice and assistance in relation to the proceedings;
- other advice or assistance in relation to the settlement or other resolution of the dispute that is the subject of the proceedings; and
- advice and assistance in relation to the enforcement of decisions in the proceedings or as part of the settlement or resolution of the dispute.

The provisions provide that advice and assistance in the form of representation and any form of dispute resolution, including mediation, may be covered by a legal services order.

### The court's approach when asked to make a legal services order

The factors to be considered by the court are:

- the court must not make a legal services order unless it is satisfied that, without the amount to be paid, the applicant would not reasonably be able to obtain appropriate legal services for the purposes of the proceedings or any part of the proceedings; and
- the court must be satisfied in particular that:
    - the applicant is not reasonably likely to be able to secure a loan to pay for the services; and
    - the applicant is unlikely to be able to obtain the services by granting a charge over any assets recovered in the proceedings.

## Things the court will consider

- Where the disclosure by the person being asked to pay is patchy/missing/not given, the court will favour the person asking for the legal services order.
- Where the person being asked to pay in the past been supported by a third party (such as mum or dad) and says that those payments have been stopped but the position of the 'supporter' is not clear, then the court is entitled to assume the 'support payments' would continue.

## Scope of the order

The scope of the order may be specified by the court and can state:

- The legal services order may be for a specified period of time or for the purposes of a specified part of the proceedings.
- It may provide for payment of all or part of the amount ordered by instalments, which may be secured; and
- payment of all or part of the amount ordered may be deferred.
- Where the main application being made appears doubtful/unlikely to succeed, the court should judge the application with caution.
- The court cannot make an order unless it is satisfied that without the payment the applicant would not reasonably be able to obtain appropriate legal services for the proceedings, and therefore the exercise essentially looks to the future.
- In determining whether the applicant can reasonably obtain funding from another source, the court would be unlikely to expect them to sell or charge their home or to deplete a modest fund of savings, although this aspect is highly fact-specific.
- Evidence of refusals by two commercial lenders of repute will normally dispose of any issue as to whether or not a litigation loan is available – so applying for two loans will deal with this point.
- In determining whether a *Sears Tooth* arrangement can be entered into, a statement of refusal by the applicant's solicitors should normally answer the question. A *Sears Tooth* agreement is where the solicitor agrees to take their payment out of the final settlement. Such agreements are rarely given nowadays and we do not offer them.
- If a litigation loan is offered at a very high rate of interest, it would be unlikely to be reasonable to expect the applicant to take it unless the respondent offered an undertaking to meet that interest.
- The order should normally contain a promise by the person getting the money that they will repay to the other any amount ordered by the court, so if at the end of the proceedings, the court says that they should repay some of the costs that they have received, they promise to do that. If they refuse to promise, it is unlikely the court would make the legal services order.
- Generally speaking, the court should not make an order to fund beyond the FDR appointment, but the court should agree to have a hearing shortly after the FDR appointment to consider further funding, if the court is asked to do so.
- When ordering costs funding for a specified period, monthly instalments are to be preferred to a single lump sum payment.

## Can it be changed/varied once made?

A legal services order may be varied at any time in the proceedings if the court considers that there has been a material change of circumstances since the order was made.

*If you need further guidance on this issue, please raise your questions with us.*

# 3 Disclosure

## 3.1 Introduction

This chapter deals with the issue of disclosure, which can be before an application is formally issued or in compliance with the directions in a Form C. This takes up a great deal of a practitioner's time in one way or another. The exchange of financial information will hopefully lead to the parties being able to negotiate a settlement. If the parties are unable to negotiate terms of settlement, the court should have sufficient information and documentation available to decide as to the financial division between the parties. The parties are usually able to reach a settlement at or after the FDR hearing at the latest.

## 3.2 Voluntary disclosure

Most solicitors will, at one time or another, agree to proceed with the process of 'voluntary disclosure'. This term is often used by solicitors without much precision and this can lead to confusion and ultimately additional expense for the client. Care should be taken to agree the form and process to be used for voluntary financial disclosure.

An updated pre-application protocol is annexed to FPR Practice Direction 9A, to take into account the changes to FPR 2010 effective from 29 April 2024.

> The Protocol sets out the key steps the court will expect parties to take in relation to non-court dispute resolution (NCDR), i.e. resolving a dispute other than through the court process, before starting court proceedings. The Protocol also underlines the duty to make full and honest disclosure. [...] Everyone is required to comply with the terms of the Protocol, even if they have not had professional advice from a legal representative.

The protocol is reproduced in full at **Annex 3G**.

There is a greater emphasis on the consideration and use of NCDR, focusing on the relevant issues and controlling costs. There is an expectation that at least one process of NCDR will have been used (pre-application protocol, summary, para.2).

The protocol 'underlines the duty of parties to make full and honest disclosure of all material facts, documents, and other information relevant to the issues' (pre-application protocol, para.3) – remember the comment earlier about applications being made often because of lack of disclosure and a copy being required to be given to a client before they make a court application (pre-application protocol, para.4). Expected efforts to resolve cases before coming to court are set out in para.6. In the current climate of heavy delays, expect that you will be asked what you as a solicitor have done to promote this with your client.

Paras.10–20 again emphasise the need to try to resolve situations without heavy engagement of the court. You must read the pre-application protocol and expect that the court and the other representative will have done so too.

In **Annex 3A** we have provided for two possible alternatives in respect of disclosure. In the first instance, we have asked the client to complete financial disclosure by way of the Form E. Although this can be time-consuming and may be costly for the client if assistance is needed to complete the form, if voluntary disclosure does not result in a settlement the Form E can be updated for the court process.

In the alternative provision, the precedent asks the client to provide the solicitor with the documentation required to produce schedules, rather than to complete the Form E. In cases where there is little money and the cost of full disclosure by the Form E would be seen to be excessive, it may be more sensible for the parties to exchange schedules of assets, liabilities, income and outgoings with select and relevant documents.

**Annex 3B** sets out the mandatory filing documents that a client is required to attach to the Form E; however, in reality the practitioner should try to tailor the requirements by deleting any documents that are not relevant.

## 3.3 Documents needed for Form E

**Annex 3B** sets out all of the documents that the client must produce when completing the Form E. As these documents must be filed when completing the form for litigation purposes, none of the items should be deleted, unless they have no direct application to the client. For example, if the client is not a business owner then box 2.11 can be deleted. The documents to be returned to the practitioner should be marked on the attached table and the client has space to make comments next to each box. If the client is waiting for a cash equivalent (CE) value of a pension, a note of the date when the request was sent to the pension trustee can be given at section 2.13. It can be quite difficult to control documents if they are sent to you in a disorganised or piecemeal fashion, and so encouraging the client to send the paperwork in one batch is quite important. It can also save them in costs.

Occasionally, you will be aware of other documents that are important in a particular case. For example, if there are two properties, one of which will be set out at section 2.2, there may be a deed of declaration of trust that must be provided. You should adapt the table to ensure that additional documents are requested in respect of each section if you are aware that such documents exist.

## 3.4 Self-help or 'smash and grab'

It is very important that clients are told at an early stage of litigation that they should not 'help themselves' to their ex-spouse's documents. Even in cases where the parties have been fairly easy-going during the marriage about accessing documents, the client needs to be warned that this should stop when divorce proceedings are started.

The leading case in this area is the Court of Appeal decision in *Tchenguiz* v. *Imerman*; *Imerman* v. *Imerman* [2010] EWCA Civ 908. The Law Society's Family Law Protocol indicates at para.10.7.2 that it is a breach of confidence for one spouse to examine, copy, retain or use a confidential document.

The Court of Appeal described confidential documents as 'communications which are concerned with an individual's private life, including his personal finances, personal business dealings, and (possibly) his other business dealings are the stuff of personal confidentiality'.

A document will be confidential if one spouse knows that the other would not want them to look at the document or have a copy of it. Simply put, one spouse should not look at documents belonging to the other unless they have been given permission to do so, for example, if the parties have exchanged documents at mediation or during the collaborative law process. The fact that the parties had previously given each other permission to look at documents cannot be relied upon if their relationship has broken down and it should be clear that such permission is withdrawn.

It is, therefore, sensible to write to the other side to withdraw such permissions given by your client. If one spouse gave the other permission to access their online banking, email accounts or other online documents then permission should specifically be withdrawn to avoid any suggestion that permission to access those documents remains post-divorce. The letters at **Annex 1M** and **Annex 3D** explain to clients that they should not give the practitioner any documents belonging to their spouse and the reasons why. A number of statutes prevent one party accessing the other's documents, see for example the data protection legislation, the Computer Misuse Act 1990 and the Postal Services Act 2000.

Where the client is concerned that their spouse will destroy documents before producing the Form E, the letter invites the client to discuss matters with the solicitor. There is a possibility that an application can be made to prevent the destruction of documents.

The best course of action is to prompt the client to change their online passwords and to ensure that they sever any iCloud or similar links with their ex-spouse's mobile devices. Although the spouse should not be looking at those documents, it is better to ensure that there is no access to them in the first place.

If the client gives the solicitor documents that do not belong to the client, the solicitor should immediately return the documents to their owner. The solicitor should not examine the documents or take a copy of them. Full disclosure of those documents should then be requested in the proper way during the proceedings.

## 3.5 Form E

The financial statement sets out the disclosure that the client is required to provide to the court. Form E is available online at **www.gov.uk/government/publications/form-e-financial-statement-for-a-financial-order-matrimonial-causes-act-1973-civil-**

**partnership-act-2004-for-financial-relief-after-an-overseas**. This is the most important document that will be produced for your client in a financial matter.

### 3.5.1 Page one

The first page of the financial statement requires the important factual information such as the names of the parties, their role within the proceedings and the date of the form.

The warning notices on the first page are very important and the client's attention should be drawn to these notices when sending the form to the client to complete. Of particular relevance is the fact that any person found to have been deliberately untruthful may have criminal proceedings brought against them under the Fraud Act 2006. The warnings also outline that proceedings for contempt of court may be brought against a person who causes a false statement to be made in a document verified by a statement of truth. In reality, it is extremely rare for criminal proceedings or contempt proceedings to be brought against a person who has deliberately lied on this financial statement.

In view of that warning, some clients will expect the court to act on inaccuracies or falsehoods or for there to be a sanction imposed but, knowing this to be unlikely, you should manage that expectation.

A list of mandatory documents that should be filed is outlined in **Annex 3B**. It is important to note that the client may attach other documents to the Form E where it is necessary to explain or clarify any information within the form. It is also good practice to include documents where these would aid understanding and clarify the content of the form and the overall financial picture of the client.

### 3.5.2 General information

The general information required on page 2 is fairly straightforward and these sections should not be left blank. Under MCA 1973, s.25(2)(d) the court is required to take into account the age of the parties and the length of the marriage. You should note that any period of cohabitation that has moved seamlessly to marriage will count towards the overall length of the marriage. Page 2 does not require any information to be inserted about the length of cohabitation, and this information should be inserted at section 4.5.

Clients sometimes express concerns about sections 1.8 and 1.9 regarding new partners or possible cohabitation in the next six months. Naturally, clients should be encouraged to be as honest as possible about their plans for the future. There is no definition of cohabitation in the Family Court, and you should take careful instructions about your client's living arrangements. If the client suddenly commences cohabitation very soon after a financial settlement, the other party may make an application to set aside the order if that party believes there has not been full and frank financial disclosure of pertinent facts. Cohabitation with a new partner rarely makes a significant impact on the division of matrimonial assets accrued during the course of the marriage.

Details of any children of the family are usually limited at section 1.10 to minor children who were children of the family, i.e. lived together with the parties of the marriage. It is, however, possible to include details of adult children, particularly where they continue to reside with one of the parties and are being supported by them. Some practitioners will include details of all children, even those who are adults and not living at home, so as to give the court more context regarding the relationship.

When giving details of the state of health of the client or the children, consideration should be given to any documents that could be attached in order to clarify any health conditions. It is good practice to give detailed information about any medication that is being taken to manage a health condition and whether any tests or diagnosis are imminent. This will minimise the enquiries raised at the questionnaire stage.

If expert medical evidence is needed this will be directed by the court, usually at the First Appointment.

MCA 1973, s.25(2)(e) requires the court to take into account any mental or physical disability of either party. It is therefore important that sufficient information is given to the court to enable this exercise to take place.

The court needs to understand the educational arrangements for the children, and this can include tertiary education for soon-to-be adult children. Although the court does not need to prioritise the welfare needs of adult children, their needs will not be wholly discounted. If the schools are fee-paying, it is worth mentioning that fact here.

If you are completing the form for the spouse who is to pay child maintenance, it is prudent to undertake a CMS calculation using the relevant website: **www.gov.uk/calculate-your-child-maintenance**.

If you are acting for the person receiving child maintenance, the sum actually being paid should be inserted, or if the parties are living together an indication of the sums or specific bills being paid by the paying party should be given. It can be unhelpful if section 1.13 is left blank or if the receiving party indicates that they are not receiving maintenance if, for example, their bills are being paid by the other party instead of a formal payment of child maintenance.

Where the application before the court is to vary a previous order, section 1.14 requires the previous order to be attached together with clarification of the parts that require variation. It should be noted that MCA 1973, s.31 deals with the variation of financial remedy orders; these are restricted to periodical payments orders or lump sum orders payable in instalments.

In section 1.15, you should insert details of any other court cases in England and Wales or abroad involving the parties. Given that the divorce proceedings will now be dealt with separately under a different 16 digit number, the details of the divorce application should be detailed here. Any criminal proceedings should also be detailed here.

In section 1.16, the present residence of the client is required together with details of the occupation of that property; for example, is the client a joint owner of the property, living with parents, or living in the property under a licence or a tenancy agreement? If there is a tenancy agreement, it may be prudent to attach a copy of that agreement to the financial statement. If you want to keep the client's address confidential, this can be marked on the form and a Form C8 uploaded to the portal, if there is a financial application underway.

### *3.5.3 Financial details*

#### Part 1 Real property (land and buildings) and personal assets

Section 2.1: the client should complete any information about the family home. If the property has been sold and the proceeds of sale are being held in an account, this information should be inserted elsewhere; however, the form can be marked that the property has been sold. It is good practice to obtain a copy of the completion statement from the conveyancing solicitor.

Although it is not mandatory to file the office copy entries from the Land Registry, it is good practice to do so. Section 2.1 requires details of the Land Registry title number and details of the mortgage company, both of which can be obtained from the Land Registry.

Details of who owns the property will be recorded on the Land Registry title but it may be that the client advises you that the beneficial interests are different. For example, the parties may have entered into a deed of declaration of trust and the client believes it reflects the beneficial interests rather than the legal title. In this case, the client's instructions should be carefully recorded and the deed should be attached to the Form E. If needed, a copy of the TR1 and/or the restriction registered to protect any trust deed can be extracted.

It is possible that the client will reveal a potential third party interest at this stage and, if so, this should be drawn to the attention of the court in the statement of issues. The court might join a third party to the proceedings if it is relevant to do so. You will certainly need to consider whether the third party needs to be invited to intervene and/or be joined as a party. A third party is only bound by the decision of the matrimonial court if they are joined as a party.

It is not uncommon for the client to hold the property with their spouse as joint tenants but to give instructions that the beneficial interests are held unequally. You should tread carefully in these cases, as it is not usual to set those arguments out on this page. The client may wish to detail any contributions to the property purchase at section 4.3 rather than set out different beneficial interests at section 2.1. You may also wish to consider extracting a copy of the TR1 used for the initial purchase, so look at which box is ticked for the declarations for the property.

The client should obtain an up-to-date mortgage redemption statement so that the correct figures can be inserted on this page together with any penalties that would fall due for an early redemption. It is possible that early advice from an independent financial adviser or a mortgage broker would be helpful at this stage, if there is a hope that the mortgage will be transferred to the client. Mortgage lending criteria have changed drastically in recent years and it is important to know whether the client can afford to take over the mortgage debt. It is possible that the client will not be permitted to take over the mortgage at all and, if so, this information needs to be found out sooner rather than later.

*Property valuation*

The valuation of the family home can be a difficult issue. If both parties live in the property they should both be able to obtain independent estate agents' valuations. If one party is excluded from the property either voluntarily or by order of the court, it may be difficult to obtain an accurate valuation. Caution should be exercised when using online valuation tools as they are not particularly accurate. It may be possible to ask an estate agent to conduct a 'drive-by' valuation or a desk top valuation, which is probably more accurate than an online tool. There is always a difference between a marketing price and the realistic sale price of a property and the client should be told this to manage their expectations. A solution to avoid conflict can be for one party to propose five agents and the other to select three agents from that group.

Neither party should go to the expense of paying for a valuation at this stage as the costs are unlikely to be recoverable; a sole party expert is not likely to be used in these proceedings. The court will usually prefer estate agents to be used, at little or no cost, rather than engaging a surveyor. It is important that both parties have an approximate idea of the value of the property as, other than their pension, this is likely to be the most valuable asset that they own.

The estimate of the costs of sale is usually a fixed percentage of the current market value of the property. Depending on the geographical location and preference of the local court, this figure can be anywhere between 2% and 3% as provided by case law. However, if a party can produce direct evidence of the cost of sale in the form of a solicitors' cost quote and estate agent commission quote, this could allow the court to use those figures rather than an estimate. The total equity in the property is calculated by deducting the costs of sale and the balance outstanding on any mortgage together with penalties. Note that there is a provision for early repayment charges to be specified so ensure that the figure given for the mortgage is net of any such charge. The equity should be divided equally between the parties in the event that they are joint owners with no other declaration of trust.

If there is a deed of declaration of trust then it is perfectly acceptable to divide the equity between the parties in accordance with that document. You should note that it is unlikely that the court will ring-fence and exclude any assets according to a deed of declaration of trust as MCA 1973, s.25 requires the court to balance all resources available to each party.

Section 2.2 is similar to section 2.1 but this pertains to other property, land or buildings either in England and Wales or abroad. This is where the details of, for example, a holiday home rental property can be input using the same guidelines as above. If Capital Gains Tax (CGT) is payable on the sale or transfer of a second property, this information should be input at section 2.10. You may need to get advice from an accountant about this.

Section 2.3 requires clients to complete information about all bank and building society accounts that they have in their sole name, in joint names with another person, or that they have held in the last 12 months but have recently closed. This also includes an account in which they have a beneficial interest. For example, if a client regularly places money in another person's account but considers the money to be theirs, the client should declare the beneficial interest.

Often parents have bank accounts on behalf of their children but the accounts are actually held in the parents' names. These accounts should be disclosed in section 2.3 but in 'the total current value of your interest' section the answer will be nil if the beneficial interest of the proceeds of the account belongs to the child and not the parent. An example is shown in **Table 3.1**. It is a good idea to put the date at which you give the balance on the account because when updating disclosure is required, this means you will know what date you need to ask for documents to be updated.

**Table 3.1:** Example of completed section 2.3

| Name of bank or building society, including branch name | Type of account (e.g. current) | Account number | Name of other account holder (if applicable) | Balance at the date of this statement | Total current value of your interest |
|---|---|---|---|---|---|
| Santander – Balance as at XX.XX.XX | Savings account for Maria Jones | 1234567 | N/A | £34,500 | Nil |
| Santander – Balance as at XX.XX.XX | Current account | 9876543 | N/A | £1,278 | £1,278 |
| Santander – Balance as at XX.XX.XX | Savings account | 6758493 | Stefan Jones | £2,000 | £1,000 |

In the case of each account careful consideration should be given to the final column, 'the total current value of your interest'. It may be that in the case of joint accounts, one party has not had access to the account for some time and therefore the balance of the account belongs to the other party. Full instructions should be taken on this point. Remember that if your client is named as a joint owner on the account they can ask for copies of statements from the bank or institution.

Section 2.4 can be quite complicated depending on the type of investments the client discloses. The paperwork associated with this section is limited to the latest statement or dividend counterfoil in respect of each investment. If the client has an investment manager, they may be able to supply a letter that outlines the investments and any particular risk/liquidity issues in connection with them. Not all investments are liquid and this will not be immediately apparent from the information required to be input at section 2.4, or even the documentation attached to that section.

Clients usually have straightforward investments, such as listed shares or ISAs, and these can be easily bought and sold subject to market variations.

Section 2.5: the client should provide all information in respect of any life insurance or endowment policy held. It may be that you need to cross-check the information given by the client against the direct debits from their bank account to ensure that all policies have been disclosed. It is good practice to obtain a letter from the insurance company to confirm that a policy has no surrender value to ensure that clear disclosure is given.

It is sensible to get an experienced independent financial adviser involved in financial planning at an early stage, particularly where there are life policies that may be kept or surrendered. Practitioners cannot give financial advice and so before any settlement is proposed the client will need to understand the financial consequences from a person who is authorised to give advice. Financial planners can also undertake cash planning, if this is needed for your client in terms of maintenance or pension income provision. This is not the same as a pension on divorce expert (PODE) report.

Section 2.6: if clients are owed any money this should be detailed here, and it is a good idea to cross-check their bank statements to ensure that they have not 'loaned' any friends or family large sums of money that do not appear in this section. If there is a loan agreement, this should be attached to the financial statement; however, it is more likely that any loans are soft debts and this should be made clear.

Section 2.7: it is not unusual for some people to hold large sums of cash and this must be disclosed.

Section 2.8 can be a little tricky if the client has personal possessions that are very valuable. At this stage, the client is only required to identify those possessions and to give an estimate of the value. Any individual items that are worth less than £500 on resale should be excluded. Valuations are required for the sale of the item second hand, not when bought as new.

If an individual item forms part of a collection that is worth more than £500, then the collection should be valued and included. Ordinarily, items of furniture and house contents are not individually worth more than £500, and it is not cost proportionate to obtain valuations for house clearance at this stage.

The client should not go to the expense of paying for an expert valuation as this is something that may need to be addressed at the First Appointment and a single joint expert instructed. It is unusual to be involved in cases that require an expert opinion in relation to section 2.8.

The client should provide values only for their chattels and not for their spouse's. There will be an opportunity to challenge their spouse's chattels valuations later in the proceedings, although it is rarely cost proportionate to do so. Note that pets are becoming increasingly valuable. You should put in here the value of a dog or other pet, which will be treated as a chattel for the purposes of addressing financial issues.

## Part 2 Capital: Liabilities and Capital Gains Tax

Section 2.9: the client is required to set out all debts owed, excluding the mortgage and overdrawn bank and building society accounts which are included elsewhere in the form.

The client should set out the nature of the liability, details of the other account holder if applicable and the total liability owed. In the final column 'total current value of your interest in the liability' there are a number of different responses that can be given.

When parties enter into a credit agreement they are each responsible for the whole debt. They may attribute the liability in shares between themselves but this does not bind the lender. This means that in respect of a joint liability the strict position is that each party is responsible for the whole debt. Often, the client does not wish to appear to take on responsibility for the whole debt in the financial statement. It may be that a note needs to be made in this section to set out the client's position, which is that the parties had always paid the liability in specified shares and that the client believes that the client should only be held responsible for a share of the debt.

In the alternative, the client could complete the final column 'total current value of your interest in the liability' to reflect the sum that the client believes is their responsibility and which reflects the agreement between the spouses. An example is shown in **Table 3.2**.

In the first entry in **Table 3.2** the client has given instructions that the client should only be responsible for half of the total liability because they believe this is fair.

In the second entry the client accepts the legal position, which is that the client is responsible for the whole debt. However there is a note that gives reasons why they do not believe they should be responsible for the debt.

In the third entry the client has given instructions that the client is only responsible for £1,000 of the debt as this is what had been verbally agreed with the spouse when the sofa was purchased.

**Table 3.2:** Examples of completed section 2.9

| Liability | Name of other account holder (if applicable) | Total liability | Total current value of your interest in the liability |
|---|---|---|---|
| DFS sofa loan | My spouse | £5,000 | £2,500 |
| DFS sofa loan | My spouse | £5,000 | £5,000* |
| DFS sofa loan | My spouse | £5,000 | £1,000 |

* Although I am liable for this debt, the sofa is in my ex-spouse's home. I have no access to the sofa and I don't think I should be held responsible to repay this debt. The monthly repayments are currently being paid from the joint account.

Any of these is potentially acceptable as long as there is an explanation at section 2.9, otherwise there are likely to be questions raised by the other party about the distribution of this joint liability.

CGT payable needs to be identified at section 2.10. It is sensible to list those assets that would incur a CGT liability if sold or transferred. In the case of real property, it may be a good idea to obtain a CGT calculation from an accountant.

If there is a complex portfolio of investments, the investment manager will usually be able to calculate CGT due if the portfolio is sold or transferred.

If there is a dispute about the CGT liability it is possible that a single joint expert will be needed to advise on CGT; thus it is initially sensible to get a calculation carried out.

## Part 3 Capital: Business assets and directorships

Section 2.11 requires the client to complete details of any business interests: this relates to sole traders, partnerships and interests in limited companies. In each case it is mandatory to attach business accounts for the last two financial years, to the extent that they exist. As sole traders do not need to file accounts it may be that their paperwork is limited to their income tax returns and tax calculation, with no formal accounts available.

A business valuation will be needed; however, in many income-producing businesses there is no inherent value to the business itself. Clients should provide any information they can. If they have an accountant, a letter from that accountant should suffice to support any valuation. It is not necessary to spend any money obtaining a formal valuation at this stage, because if there is any dispute as to the value of the business a single joint expert will be appointed.

If there is any CGT to pay, the accountant should estimate the amount and the information should be inserted in this section. If the client does not have sufficient information to complete this section, the client should contact an accountant. It is not the solicitor's job to decipher the client's business dealings.

If the company is a limited company, quite a lot of information is available for free via the Companies House website, at **www.gov.uk/government/organisations/companies-house.** It is a good idea to check this website for information about your clients' companies or those of their spouses.

Section 2.12 is easily completed by the practitioner, who can access the Companies House website and undertake a director's search without charge.

## Part 4 Capital: Pensions and Pension Protection Fund (PPF) compensation

The issue of pensions can be a daunting one for practitioners, but the information required in the Form E is fairly straightforward. Section 2.13 should be completed for each pension that the client has, and this should be totalled to a final composite figure.

A state pension forecast can be obtained online by the client. The basic state pension figure can be sourced from the internet. If the state pension forecast for your client is below the minimum, it is worth asking your client to obtain a figure for the amount required to repair their national insurance record.

If your client's state pension forecast is higher than the basic state pension, your client may have an element of protected pension, rolled over from the former Additional State Pension, and this can be the subject of a pension sharing order. The basic state pension cannot be shared.

When completing the valuation requests in respect of state pension schemes, it is important to note whether the petition was filed before 6 April 2016 or after that date. The client should be specifically advised to put the date of the petition in the form, otherwise the Department for Work and Pensions will assume that the petition was issued after 6 April 2016 when the new scheme came into effect.

All other pensions should be included, which includes any pension that is being administered by the Pension Protection Fund (PPF) (or is in the PPF assessment period); the client should be aware if their pension has been taken on by the PPF. The PPF keeps a full list of pensions have been transferred to it – see **www.ppf.co.uk/schemes**.

The client should contact the pension trustees or the board of the PPF as soon as possible so that there is enough time to obtain the CE value. Many schemes can take three months to produce a CE valuation and so it is imperative that early enquiries are made. If the pension is in payment, the pension fund administrators may ask for a fee for calculating the CE value.

When the information is returned by the pension trustees for the PPF, it should be possible to complete section 2.13 with full information. The information provided for divorce purposes will indicate whether the occupational pension is paying reduced CEs. This is also true of underfunded schemes, where the trustees must offer shadow membership as an implementation option.

The pension valuations should always be dated within the last 12 months; if not, a further valuation should be requested. Most pension schemes will provide one CE without cost every 12 months. If the member is drawing the pension, or is within 12 months of doing so, the administrators may charge for providing the CE.

There is sometimes a misconception that a pension in payment cannot have a valuation, but this is not the case. Often, there will be an administration charge to the member to obtain a CE for a pension in payment. These costs can be quite high, particularly for government pension schemes.

If the pension valuation is not available when the Form E is completed, the information should be obtained as soon as possible and filed with the court and the other side when it is received. FPR 2010, rule 9.14 states that if a party is unavoidably prevented from sending a document required by the financial statement, i.e. the pension valuation, that party must send a copy of the document to the other party and the court as soon as possible. When the document is sent to the court, the party must provide a written explanation of the failure to send that document with the financial statement. This is an important provision which is often overlooked by practitioners.

## Part 5 Capital: Other assets

Section 2.14 is an all-encompassing section, covering any other investments or assets that have not yet been disclosed. The list at the beginning of the section is not exhaustive and clients should be reminded that any asset, interest in a trust or anything of value in England and Wales or abroad should be included. It may be that the client is the beneficiary of a discretionary trust and that this information will need to be input. Once again, if there is an investment manager who is able to assist in the preparation of the Form E, their advice should be sought at an early stage.

Sometimes clients will want to know whether they need to include an inheritance that they may come into in the future. Generally speaking, this is not necessary because if testators are still alive then there is no guarantee that their wills will remain the same until death. There is also no guarantee that there will be any money in the estate at the point of death. However, if somebody is the ultimate beneficiary of a will trust then this is something that should be disclosed.

## Part 6 Income: Earned income from employment

The information in section 2.15 can be completed using the P60 and the last three payslips, which must be filed with the Form E in any event. If the client works shift patterns, the most recent payslips will assist in calculating an average monthly sum that the client is paid. This will help to ascertain the future net income in the next 12 months and whether there is any surplus income at the end of the month after the payment of outgoings.

Using the client's payslips, an explanation should be provided as to any additional deductions, for example for travel expenses or pension contributions. If the payslips are not an accurate reflection of the normal income then a full explanation should be given. If there are any bonuses or other occasional payments these should also be indicated, as an accurate picture of the client's income is needed. It is most important in this part of the form to provide an accurate estimate of the net income in this employment for the next 12 months. If the figure is significantly different from the net income figure for the last 12 months, whether higher or lower, full explanation needs to be given in box 4.1.2, but this is sometimes forgotten by practitioners. For example, if the client has recently started, or is about to start, a new job, this may be an explanation for a change in estimated net income.

If the client has disclosed a business interest in a limited company, the client will often be receiving a small income as PAYE income which represents their director's remuneration. The majority of their income from that company will be received by way of dividend payments on their shares. If your client has changed employment during the previous 12 months, do not forget to ask for a copy of the P45. If there has been a redundancy payment, you should ask for a copy of the redundancy payment statement and, if there is one, a copy of the settlement agreement.

## Part 7 Income: Income from self-employment or partnership

Even if clients have already disclosed a business interest, they will still need to complete section 2.16 of the Form E to disclose their income from that business. Once again, this section can probably be completed by their accountant. A copy of the last tax assessment will be needed to ascertain the client's tax liability.

Ordinarily, the last tax return rather than the tax assessment is attached. Often, if only the tax assessment is attached, the other side will ask for a copy of the last tax return to ensure that all income has been declared. It is important to estimate the net annual income for the next 12 months as accurately as possible. If the figure is different from the previous year's net income, an explanation should be given on page 15 where requested.

## Part 8 Income: Income from investments

In section 2.17 you must cross-reference the earlier sections of the Form E which may have referred to income-producing investments (sections 2.2, 2.4 and 2.14). Clients often forget to disclose the income from these investments and this can lead to further questions being raised in the questionnaire. Although no further evidence needs to be provided to support the additional income, there is likely to be evidence of deposits into the disclosed bank statements. It is important to provide an accurate estimate of income for the next 12 months. If there is an investment manager dealing with a portfolio of investments, the manager may be able to give an estimate of investment income.

Clients should not forget to disclose any income from a second property, or even from renting a room in their property. Remember that tax is payable on this income.

## Part 9 Income: Income from state benefits

When completing section 2.18 it is important to note that tax credits or universal credit are not classified as state benefits, as they are paid by HMRC not the Department of Work and Pensions. If the client is entitled to child benefit, personal independence payments or state pension payments these should be included, together with any other benefits.

## Part 10 Income: Any other income

Income from a private pension or compensation received from the PPF should be included in section 2.19. Often there is documentary evidence to support these payments and although it is not mandatory to file that information, it is good practice to do so.

All tax credits can be inserted into this section. Tax credits are being phased out and migrated to universal credit.

If the client is receiving child maintenance, this should be included here. It may have been mentioned in section 1.13 but the income sections calculate the complete net income figure and the information in earlier sections is therefore not included.

If the client is receiving housekeeping money from an adult child, this should be included here. Any other income, for example royalties, not previously disclosed should be disclosed in this section and an estimated net income figure for the next 12 months should be provided.

Although the form suggests that figures can be given gross or net, it is much more helpful for net figures to be used throughout.

If a child in the household of the client is receiving disability living allowance, the income belongs to the child and should not be recorded in this statement.

## Summaries

If you are using good Form E software, the summaries page will self-calculate. If you are using the Form E provided at **www.gov.uk/government/publications/form-e-financial-statement-for-a-financial-order-matrimonial-causes-act-1973-civil-partnership-act-2004-for-financial-relief-after-an-overseas**, then sections 2.20 and 2.21 should be carefully added up to ensure that the calculations are correct. The summary pages are not particularly useful in practice, but do need to be correct.

### *3.5.4 Financial requirements*

## Part 1 Income needs

Section 3.1 requires the client to indicate whether income needs are being set out as weekly, monthly or annual figures. It does not matter which the client uses but the periods should be consistent. Most practitioners set out monthly figures rather than weekly or annual figures.

In the section starting 'I anticipate my income needs are going to change because' the client should insert an explanation as to how their current costs and estimated future costs are likely to differ. For example, the client may currently be in rented accommodation and hope to be able to purchase a house after the financial remedy proceedings have concluded.

It may be that the client is housed in a property that is too big for their current needs and so the client is likely to sell the property and purchase a smaller property which should be cheaper to maintain. A realistic approach needs to be taken in this section and when setting out the estimate of income needs at section 3.1.1.

If the client does not wish to move from the current home, current and estimated future costs will not vary greatly. It may be that some items of expenditure will change due to natural price increases, such as the cost of petrol, electricity and gas. The client may, for example, be on a fixed-rate mortgage deal which is due to come to an end in the next 6 to 12 months and a new estimate may be provided for mortgage payments thereafter. The client must be able to justify any difference between the two columns at section 3.1.1.

The Excel spreadsheet at **Annex 3C** sets out an easy-to-follow format for the client to complete. This is presented as a spreadsheet rather than a Word document as this will be much easier to amend/update as the case goes on.

**Annex 3C** is divided into sections:

1A Housing – main home.
IB Housing – second/other property.
2 Food and household.
3 Clothes, footwear, etc.
4 Other expenses.
5 Help in the house.
6 Car and other transport.
7 Personal expenditure.
8 Entertainment, hobbies, holidays.
9 Insurance and savings.
10 Employment expenses.
11 Miscellaneous.

*Children:*

12 Education for children.
13 Clothing and footwear for children.
14 Activities, holidays for children.
15 Miscellaneous for children.

Each subsection is totalled in respect of both current and estimated future costs. There is also a total for the client's expenses and a grand total to include all income needs. The grand total figure is the sum that should be inserted on page 20 of the Form E.

Any additional items can be added to the schedule to ensure that it is appropriate for the client and the children. The schedule will be the basis for any maintenance claim, or if completed by the paying party will inform the court whether there is any surplus income once their outgoings have been paid.

You should be aware of the impact of this exercise and use your experience to discourage the use of unrealistic figures – either too high or too modest. The budget is intended to inform the court and so needs to be as accurate as possible.

If you use an Excel spreadsheet, you should remember to insert the pages into the Form E and not have it as an additional document. It can so easily be lost.

## Part 2 Capital needs

Section 3.2 requires the client to complete information about capital needs for themselves and for their children (if any). Capital needs are primarily centred on housing and any improvement to housing that is needed. Therefore the main item in section 3.2.1 will be a property to live in. It is a good idea to indicate the size of property being sought and the geographical location in which that property is required. Often the client would like to remain living in the property that was the family home; if so, this is usually input together with a value of the family home.

In the event that a different property will be required for housing, the additional costs of purchase and stamp duty and moving will need to be included. If the new property needs renovating, furnishing and carpeting, these costs should be included.

Occasionally there are other capital needs, for example, the cost of a car or other equipment that is necessary for the client.

Capital needs for children are limited; however, school fees might be paid from capital and therefore included at section 3.2.2 rather than at 3.1.2. Sometimes children have capital needs for sports equipment or equipment to support a disability. If there is a need or desire for one parent to assist an adult child to pay university tuition fees this should be included here.

### GENERAL

The information in section 4 should be completed very carefully as this is the information that the court will use to assess the merits of the claim. Naturally, as the litigation progresses, information can be expanded upon if directions are given to allow the filing of statements or the additional filing of evidence. However, you should use these sections to ensure that all of the information that you hope to rely on is included from the outset. This means that detailed instructions need to be taken about all of the matters included.

Many of the items covered in this section correlate to MCA 1973, s.25; therefore, it is imperative that the information is as full as possible.

Section 4.1.1 asks the client to detail any significant changes in assets or income in the last 12 months. If capital has been utilised for legitimate reasons, for example the payment of legal costs, then it is fully transparent to include those capital payments in this section. If income has increased or decreased in the last 12 months, this is the place to include that information and provide any evidence if it assists.

Likewise, any anticipated changes in assets or income in the next 12 months should be detailed at section 4.1.2. Thus, for example, if the client is likely to drawdown a pension lump sum then this must be highlighted so that appropriate safeguards can be put in place, if necessary, to prevent a disposition of this money. If there is likely to be a significant change in income in the next 12 months, this may have been noted at section 2.15 and a full explanation can be given here.

### STANDARD OF LIVING

Section 4.2 reflects MCA 1973, s.25(2)(c). This requires the court to take into account the standard of living enjoyed by the family before the breakdown of the marriage. Whether your client is a high net worth individual or someone with average assets and income, this section must be completed. The following phrases are often seen in this section:

> The parties lived a fair standard of living, they both worked during their marriage and claimed child benefit and tax credits. They were able to enjoy a caravan holiday every year and have not been abroad since before the children were born.

Or perhaps if the parties enjoyed a better standard of living this may be typical:

> The parties enjoyed a very good standard of living as the wife has a very well paid job. Husband has not needed to work and has stayed at home with the children of the family. The parties enjoy three foreign holidays a year, a skiing holiday in the winter, a beach holiday in the summer and at least one city break during the year. The children both attend private fee-paying schools. The parties have a cleaner and gardener and enjoy the use of a part-time cook during the week.

### CONTRIBUTIONS

Section 4.3 deals with any particular contributions that one party has made to the family property and assets or outgoings or to family life or to the welfare of the family. This section reflects MCA 1973, s.25(2)(f), which states that the court must have regard to 'the contributions which each of the parties has made or is likely in the foreseeable future to make to the welfare of the family, including any contribution by looking after the home or caring for the family'.

It may be that one party wishes to emphasise financial contributions made to the purchase of the family home. The asset is disclosed at section 2.1 but if it is owned in joint tenancy, the equity will be divided equally at total A. The client may wish to persuade the court that the equity should not be distributed in accordance with legal ownership, so this section needs to be completed in full. If the client has any evidence to support this position, this evidence should be attached to the Form E, otherwise further questions will be raised in the questionnaire about the financial contributions.

This section should be completed in light of the House of Lords judgment in the case of *White* v. *White* [2000] UKHL 54. This case indicates that although the parties to the marriage may have different roles – often one is the wage earner and the other is the homemaker – their contributions will be treated as equal even though these contributions are of a different nature.

The court will look at one party's contributions and may distribute the assets to take those contributions into account.

### CONDUCT

Section 4.4 should only be completed by the client in rare circumstances. This section mirrors MCA 1973, s.25(2)(g), which says that the court must have regard to 'the conduct of each of the parties, if that conduct is such that it would in the opinion of the court be inequitable to disregard it'.

The leading case on conduct is *Miller* v. *Miller; McFarlane* v. *McFarlane* [2006] UKHL 24. This identifies that the conduct argument should be used in only the most exceptional cases. In those cases the conduct will be 'obvious and gross'.

Domestic abuse, financial control and coercive control may be relevant to your case. However, this could also be recited in section 4.3 of the Form E. Cases where conduct is such a feature that it would impact the financial distribution are rare, though there was a recent case, *N* v. *J* [2024] EWFC 184, which addressed the interplay of conduct and domestic abuse. It is expected that this issue, in the context of financial cases, will be further considered as the understanding and impact of financial abuse and coercive control are further understood.

If this section is completed frivolously then it can lead to accusations that the maker of the statement has embarked on a course of litigation conduct. District judges do not take kindly to these sections being completed when they should not be. Clients should be made aware of the serious consequences of completing this section improperly.

### ANY OTHER CIRCUMSTANCES

Section 4.5 allows the client to include any other circumstances that have not yet been mentioned that may significantly affect the extent of financial provision. This reflects the provision at MCA 1973, s.25(1): the court shall have regard to all of the circumstances of the case.

There is a list of matters that may be applicable, and anything that the client has not yet covered can be input here. As noted above, any significant period of premarital cohabitation should be mentioned here.

### 3.5.5 *Other information*

Section 4.6 specifically asks for information about the client's new relationship, if any, and asks for information about the new partner's income, assets and liabilities. It is helpful for the client to provide this information, as failure to do so can heighten distrust between the parties, which will impact negatively on the possibility of settling matters.

### 3.5.6 *Order sought*

It may be too soon to be able to complete this section but you should attempt to present a transparent position for your client.

If the client hopes to remain in the family home, this should be stated in section 5.1(a) so that proper directions can be given to investigate the possibility of releasing the other party from any mortgage covenants. It should be made clear whether a sale of the family home is sought.

You should know whether continuing spousal maintenance is sought (section 5.1(b)), even if it is too soon to know if there is sufficient income to meet this need.

If there has been no pre-litigation disclosure, the client might not yet have sufficient information regarding their spouse's pension situation when answering section 5.1(c). Therefore the answer to this section might be a little more vague.

Section 5.2 relates to applications for a variation of an ante-nuptial or post-nuptial settlement and, if such a variation is sought, the settlement needs to be identified.

If there is an application for an avoidance of disposition order, section 5.3 needs to be completed to identify the property to which the disposition relates. In such cases the party to whom the disposition was made must be served with a copy of the application and they can request a copy of the financial statement within 14 days of service (FPR 2010, rule 9.13(4)).

### 3.5.7 *Statement of truth*

Although the statement of truth can be signed by the solicitor, it is preferable if it is signed by the client. FPR 2010, Part 17 and Practice Direction 17A deal with the practice rules regarding statements of truth.

Paragraph 3.8 of Practice Direction 17A states that where a legal representative signs the statement of truth, this signature will be taken by the court as the legal representative's statement that the legal representative has authority to sign the statement of truth. You should be careful to obtain authority before signing the Form E.

It is also an indication that you explained to the client that in signing the statement of truth, the client was confirming that it was the client's belief that the facts in the document were true.

You will also be taken to have explained the possible consequences if it subsequently appears that the client did not have an honest belief in the truth of those facts.

### *3.5.8 Schedule of documents to accompany the Form E*

These documents are the mandatory filing documents that the client is required to submit. It is good practice to complete this page to indicate which documents are attached.

However, in addition to completing this section it is good practice to produce an index page appended to the front of the documents. This sets out the documents attached, the sections that the documents relate to, and the date(s) of the documents.

This practice accords with the provisions of FPR 2010, Practice Direction 22A, para.11.3:

> Where an exhibit contains more than one document, a front page should be attached setting out a list of the documents contained in the exhibit. The list should contain the dates of the documents.

**Annex 3B** includes a template for the list of documents that should accompany the Form E. Most solicitors now have bundling software and this can be used very effectively to produce the exhibit bundle of documents. It is best for the Form E and the exhibit bundle to be separately produced. This aids preparation of a hearing bundle later in the case.

The Form E should be signed by the party who is making the statement. Practitioners should avoid signing this document. A document signed electronically via a digital packet is acceptable.

Whether the Form E is being prepared for voluntary disclosure or for a formal court application, it is helpful for you to ask your client to produce sample property particulars. In a contested format, this will be required to comply with the Efficiency Statement.

In a contested application, the Form E and exhibit bundle should be uploaded to the portal. Do not mark the document as confidential or it cannot be shared. The respondent cannot 'see' the document in the portal until you share the document. Do not mark the Form E and exhibit as being for the FDR or it will be placed on the FDR tab within the portal and the judge will not be able to see it at the First Appointment. There are no file size limits for the upload.

## 3.6 Schedule of outgoings

It is important for every practitioner to have access to a good schedule of outgoings to give the client as a precedent. Therefore **Annex 3C** is an Excel spreadsheet for the client to complete or for you to complete with the client. Many schedule of outgoings documents are created as Word documents, which may be easier for the client to complete than an Excel spreadsheet. However, using a spreadsheet will make it easier to update the information if the client's situation changes if automatic calculations are inserted.

## 3.7 After the exchange of Form E

The letter at **Annex 3E** sets out those matters that should be explained to clients when sending them their spouse's Form E. Obviously, there is a limited time within which to prepare the following documents in readiness for the First Appointment:

1. Request for further information and documentation, otherwise known as 'the questionnaire'.
2. Form ES1.
3. Form ES2.
4. Form G (this indicates whether the parties are in a position to use the first directions appointment as a financial dispute resolution hearing).
5. Property particulars suitable for your client (maximum of three).
6. Property particulars suitable for the other party (maximum of three).
7. Mortgage capacity information to be obtained jointly, unless a reason can be given otherwise.
8. Form H.

Generally, you can start to draft the documents without any input from the client; however, the client's input will be needed before the documentation can be exchanged with the other side.

There is a tension between FPR 2010 and the Efficiency Statement. The documents required, at the time of writing (July 2024), are those set out in the Efficiency Statement. The Family Procedure Rules Committee has issued a consultation regarding possible amendment of Practice Direction 27A to take account of the Efficiency Statement and the President's guidance on electronic bundling (see **4.2**).

The ES1 and ES2 templates are available on the judicial website. The ES2 is in an Excel spreadsheet with automatic calculations. The figures do not need to be agreed. The applicant puts their figures in one column and the respondent uses their own column. Judges find it helpful for the disputed 'lines' to be highlighted in yellow so that they can see discrepancies.

Remember that your client needs to have seen the Form H before it is filed.

## 3.8 Questionnaire

FPR 2010, rule 9.14(5) states that a questionnaire must be prepared, setting out by reference to the statement of issues any further information and documents requested from the other party. Generally speaking, only one document is prepared, which is referred to as 'the questionnaire'. This incorporates a request for information from the other party by way of a narrative response, and documentation that the other party is required to produce.

When considering whether a questionnaire is needed, you should remember that questions should be focused to issues that will assist the court in resolving the dispute between the parties. A questionnaire should be sent to the client to approve, to ensure that you are not asking questions that the client already knows the answer to. It should be borne in mind that every question asked has a cost for the client asking it, there is a cost to the client for answering it and a further cost for the client for you having to consider the answer.

You should be very careful when drafting the questionnaire to ensure that it is very clear whether information or documents, or both, is required. Occasionally no questions need to be raised and if this is the case the parties are probably ready to use the First Appointment as a dispute resolution hearing.

Cross-examination questions should not be asked in the questionnaire. The purpose of this document is to complete or clarify disclosure.

Any directions sought or valuations needed should be mentioned in the Form ES1 and not raised as questions in the questionnaire.

Remember that the court controls the evidence in financial remedy applications. The court must give permission for the questionnaire to be raised in the first instance, and then will consider whether each question itself should be raised.

It can be helpful for the court for you to annotate the questionnaire of the other party indicating whether or not you accept that a question should be answered, and if not, why not. That can cut down the process for the court and save time. You should serve and upload your annotated document if you choose to do this.

The court will set the time to be allowed for replies to be given. Note also that any replies must be verified with a statement of truth.

## 3.9 Form ES1

Form ES1 is a template document referenced in the Efficiency Statement. It is straightforward to complete. The last section should be focused on what the court needs to know in respect of directions to be made at the First Appointment. This document should be agreed between the solicitors for the parties and any disputed areas highlighted for the judge.

## 3.10 Form ES2

Form ES2 is another form produced alongside the Efficiency Statement and can be downloaded from the judiciary website. This is an Excel spreadsheet with calculations included. There are three columns – one for the applicant, one for the respondent and one marked 'joint'. The columns are then further subdivided allowing for the applicant's figures and the respondent's figures. There is no need for the applicant to agree the respondent's figures and vice versa. If the figures do not match, the disputed figures should be highlighted in yellow to assist the judge.

## 3.11 Conclusion

This chapter covers a lot of ground regarding disclosure obligations before the first hearing when disclosure is the main focus of preparation. The duty of full and frank disclosure to the court is ongoing and this should be kept in mind by you and your client. The obligation should be explained to the client and they should be asked to notify you as soon as any change in their financial situation occurs.

# Annex 3A

## Letter explaining information required for voluntary disclosure

Dear [*name of client*]

As you know we have agreed with [*name of spouse*]'s solicitor that we are going to proceed with 'voluntary disclosure'. Disclosure is the process whereby each party collects their financial information for the purpose of swapping that information with the other party.

We have agreed to do this and then try to negotiate a settlement. If this process works, there will be no need to start court proceedings. We will, however, need to send a draft consent order to the court for the judge to approve the terms of settlement. The judge has the power to accept or reject a settlement. If the settlement is fair to both parties, the judge will accept it and make an order.

One of the potential pitfalls of proceeding with voluntary disclosure is that the parties sometimes take a very long time to prepare the financial information needed. Obviously, the longer you take to give me your financial information, the longer it will be before negotiations can start.

### Timetable

With voluntary disclosure it is important that you understand that although there is no specific timetable to adhere to, it is important that we try to exchange financial information as quickly as possible. We will usually agree a date to work towards and so we need to know from you how long it will take you to gather the information and documents together.

In court proceedings, we would have 8 to 12 weeks to complete the financial disclosure form, known as the 'Form E'. In my experience, if we take a long time preparing the financial information, any drive to move negotiations on may be lost, so if you could come back to me as soon as possible to tell me how long you need, that would be helpful.

### *Option A: Form E disclosure – the statement*

In this case we have agreed to exchange financial information by using the Form E as a guide. The Form E gives the information and the documents supporting the Form E verify the information given in the Form E.

The process I prefer to use is:

- You to send me your documentation and information.
- I will prepare a draft of your Form E.

- We will work together to get the Form E in a final state that you are happy with and that is accurate.

**[If the practitioner has agreed to exchange financial information by way of schedules with supporting documents, it is sensible to send the following to the client. Be aware that information can be missed if using a schedule and so the preference would be to use the Form E.]**

### *Option B: Disclosure by schedules*

I will be collating the documentation you send me into a format with a schedule to clearly explain the information.

### Information and documentation needed from you

I have attached for you:

1. a leaflet setting out the documentation that I need from you;
2. a budget form in an Excel spreadsheet format for you to use. This form will be used to show what you are actually spending now out of your income and what you think your future expenses will be, when you are settled into your new home.

It is more cost effective for you to gather your information and send it to me in one packet, rather than piece by piece.

If you have any questions, please do contact me. If you could come back to me with the date by which you think you can gather your information, that would be helpful.

# Annex 3B

## Guidance to client for production of Form E documents

The court rules require that you must enclose with the Form E copies of the following documents (and you should consider assets in this country and worldwide):

1. Valuations for any properties you own. If you have not had a formal valuation, please would you ask three estate agents to value the properties or alternatively find similar properties on the RightMove or Zoopla websites to give an idea of value. If you rent your property, I need a copy of your tenancy agreement. Please do not use 'average' value calculations since those are often inaccurate.
2. A redemption statement from each of your mortgage companies, if applicable. You will need to ask them for this. This is a statement showing the amount that they would have to be paid if the mortgage were to be paid off in full. This is not the same as the annual mortgage statement. It should also state clearly any mortgage redemption penalties that apply to your mortgage. This is needed so we can work out how much equity there is in your property. You will need to do this for any mortgages you have.
3. Statements of account for all bank, building society and NS&I accounts, which are in credit, which you hold or have an interest in (including ISAs) covering the last 12 months. Please also include any PayPal accounts. You need to include any accounts that you have held in the last 12-month period, even if they are now closed. For example, if you closed a bank account 6 months ago, you still need to produce bank account statements for that account. If you do not have a full 12 months' worth of statements, then you must ask the bank or building society for further copies. The same will apply if any are missing. It is much cheaper and more time effective for you to do this now, rather than have requests for production at a later date. Please also include company or business bank accounts which might not be in your name but in respect of which you have full control. If you hold any crypto assets such as Bitcoin, information on this should also be provided.
4. A surrender value quotation for any life policies you hold. You will probably need to ask the life company for this. Some life policies only pay out on death and have no investment value but I still need details of those.
5. If you have a pension, a valuation of your pension rights for the purpose of matrimonial proceedings, to include a Cash Equivalent Value (a CEV). You must contact your pension provider in writing to ask for this. They will also send out the mandatory information required in financial proceedings in connection with divorce. Please would you let me have a copy of the letter you send. If you are not sure what you need to ask for, please provide me with the name of the pension provider, the fund number and a letter addressed to the pension provider authorising them to provide me with information. I can then make the request on your behalf.
6. Please also apply for a State Pension Forecast and give me a copy of the result. You can apply for this online at: **www.gov.uk/check-state-pension**.
7. If you are an employee, please provide your last three payslips and your P60 for the most recently completed financial year. Please also let me have your P11D if you receive benefits in kind, such as health care, a season ticket loan etc.

8. If you are a director of a limited company or in a business partnership, the last two years' accounts, your last two years' tax returns and the tax calculations for the last two years so that your net income can be calculated. If your year end has passed and your accounts have not been finalised, please ask your accountant to complete this work. You would be expected to do so for the purposes of any court proceedings.
9. Proof of income from any other source, e.g. dividend payments on shares, rent from a property, child maintenance from your partner/former partner.
10. If you receive child benefit, tax credits, a state pension or any other benefits, copies of your benefit award letter or a screenshot from the Universal Credit award.
11. Any child maintenance assessment letter or agreement.
12. Copies of any Premium Bonds you hold and a letter stating whether you have won any prizes in the last 12 months.
13. Copies of share certificates showing any shareholdings that you have.
14. A value for any car you own and if it is subject to a finance agreement, a copy of the finance agreement. Using a website such as WeBuyAnyCar.com to value is fine.
15. Your valuation for any contents of the property or items of contents/jewellery, etc. worth more than £500 – this may include laptops, phones, bikes, etc.
16. Details of any debts, both joint and in your own name, with documentary proof of these debts, such as credit card statements or a letter from a family member who has loaned you money.
17. The attached income and expenditure budget duly completed. Please enter monthly figures. This is meant to be an estimate of what it will cost for you to run the home that you eventually end up living in.

Most people find the budget forms to be a little tricky. You can enter the figures that you know you are paying or will have to pay, and you can also enter figures for things that maybe you cannot afford now but that would be reasonable for you to have. Holidays are a prime example of this. If income/money is tighter than usual, then most people will divert income to the essentials and put a holiday to one side. You can enter items that it would be reasonable or fair to have to show a true picture of your income needs moving forward. You also need to include **everything** so please do complete the budget form fully.

When you give financial disclosure, the aim is to give a full, frank and clear financial picture of what you have. It covers property and money held in this country and abroad. It is only once there is a good clear picture of what family assets there are and what their value is that it will be possible to begin to analyse the figures and look at what is a reasonable settlement.

Although we give financial disclosure now, **there is a continuing obligation to give disclosure**. This means you need to keep saving your bank statements and other financial paperwork as it may be called for further along in your case. You also need to let me know of any changes in your financial situation, whether this is an improvement or not.

If in doubt, tell me about it and I can advise you.

# Annex 3C

## Your expenditure

You do not need to complete every box. This form is meant to jog your memory regarding what you are spending.

| Item | What you are paying now | What you estimate you will pay in the future | Notes/ comments |
|---|---|---|---|
| **SECTION 1A: Housing – main home** | | | |
| Mortgage instalments | | | |
| Rent | | | |
| Ground rent | | | |
| Service charge | | | |
| Life insurance | | | |
| Residents' association | | | |
| Council tax | | | |
| Gas | | | |
| Electricity | | | |
| Other fuel: Calor Gas, oil, wood, coal | | | |
| Water rates | | | |
| Sewerage charge | | | |
| General maintenance, repairs, decorations | | | |
| Boiler – servicing and maintenance | | | |
| Insurance – please specify | | | |
| Building insurance | | | |
| Contents insurance | | | |
| Burglar alarms | | | |
| Garden maintenance | | | |
| Other – please specify | | | |
| Total | 0 | 0 | |
| **SECTION 1B: Housing – second/other property** | | | |
| Mortgage instalments | | | |
| Rent | | | |
| Ground rent | | | |
| Service charge | | | |
| Life insurance | | | |

| Item | What you are paying now | What you estimate you will pay in the future | Notes/ comments |
|---|---|---|---|
| Residents' association | | | |
| Council tax | | | |
| Gas | | | |
| Electricity | | | |
| Other fuel: Calor Gas, oil, wood, coal | | | |
| Water rates | | | |
| Sewerage charge | | | |
| General maintenance, repairs, decorations | | | |
| Boiler – servicing and maintenance | | | |
| Insurance – please specify | | | |
| Building insurance | | | |
| Contents insurance | | | |
| Burglar alarms | | | |
| Garden maintenance | | | |
| Other – please specify | | | |
| Total | 0 | 0 | |
| **SECTION 2: Food and household** | | | |
| Supermarket | | | |
| Additional food – specify | | | |
| Entertaining | | | |
| Christmas/religious festivals | | | |
| Hardware/cleaning materials/other | | | |
| Any other not included | | | |
| Total | 0 | 0 | |
| **SECTION 3: Clothes, footwear etc.** | | | |
| Clothes | | | |
| Sports clothes | | | |
| Footwear | | | |
| Sports footwear | | | |
| Jewellery | | | |
| Handbags | | | |
| Coats | | | |
| Other accessories | | | |

| Item | What you are paying now | What you estimate you will pay in the future | Notes/ comments |
|---|---|---|---|
| Other – specify | | | |
| Total | 0 | 0 | |
| **SECTION 4: Other expenses** | | | |
| Telephone – domestic | | | |
| Mobile telephone | | | |
| Computer maintenance, repairs, etc. | | | |
| Internet/broadband | | | |
| Software subscriptions – anti-virus/firewall | | | |
| TV licence | | | |
| Sky/cable | | | |
| Netflix, etc. | | | |
| Amazon Prime | | | |
| Apple music/Spotify, etc. | | | |
| Postage | | | |
| Laundry/dry cleaning/shoe repairs | | | |
| Stationery | | | |
| Vet bills | | | |
| Kennel/grooming, etc. | | | |
| Pet insurance | | | |
| Other – specify | | | |
| Total | 0 | 0 | |
| **SECTION 5: Help in the house** | | | |
| Cleaner | | | |
| Gardener | | | |
| Window cleaner | | | |
| Handyman | | | |
| Babysitter/childcare | | | |
| Other – specify | | | |
| Total | 0 | 0 | |
| **SECTION 6: Car and other transport** | | | |
| Road tax | | | |
| Insurance | | | |
| Servicing, maintenance and repairs | | | |

| Item | What you are paying now | What you estimate you will pay in the future | Notes/ comments |
|---|---|---|---|
| Petrol/diesel and oil | | | |
| Car wash/valet | | | |
| Congestion charge | | | |
| Parking expenses | | | |
| RAC/AA/Green Flag, etc. | | | |
| Vehicle lease | | | |
| Non-private expenses, e.g. train, taxi | | | |
| Other – specify | | | |
| Total | 0 | 0 | |
| **SECTION 7: Personal expenditure** | | | |
| Hairdressing | | | |
| Optician | | | |
| Beautician | | | |
| Cosmetics and toiletries | | | |
| Health club/gym/personal trainer | | | |
| Tobacco | | | |
| Dentist/hygienist | | | |
| Medical expenses | | | |
| Private medical, e.g. BUPA | | | |
| Chemist/pharmaceutical expenses | | | |
| Pocket money for personal items | | | |
| Total | 0 | 0 | |
| **SECTION 8: Entertainment, hobbies, holidays** | | | |
| Restaurant meals | | | |
| Theatre, cinema, concerts | | | |
| Museums, exhibitions, fairs | | | |
| Other spectator events, e.g. sports | | | |
| Books/CDs/DVDs, etc. | | | |
| Evening and other classes/workshop fees | | | |
| Hobby equipment, e.g. golf clubs | | | |
| Holiday – cost for you only | | | |
| Christmas expenses excluding food | | | |
| Birthday and other gifts, parties, etc. | | | |

| Item | What you are paying now | What you estimate you will pay in the future | Notes/ comments |
|---|---|---|---|
| Other – specify | | | |
| Total | 0 | 0 | |
| **SECTION 9: Insurance and savings** | | | |
| Life insurance | | | |
| Family protection insurance | | | |
| Mortgage protection insurance | | | |
| Sickness and accident insurance | | | |
| Other insurance | | | |
| Travel insurance | | | |
| Regular savings | | | |
| Pension contributions – not taken from wages | | | |
| Other – specify | | | |
| Total | 0 | 0 | |
| **SECTION 10: Employment expenses** | | | |
| Travel expenses | | | |
| Lunches | | | |
| Special clothing, footwear, equipment | | | |
| Subscriptions | | | |
| Professional associations | | | |
| Union fees | | | |
| Other – specify | | | |
| Total | 0 | 0 | |
| **SECTON 11: Miscellaneous** | | | |
| Donations to charities, churches, etc. | | | |
| Bank charges | | | |
| Loan repayments or credit charges | | | |
| Other items not elsewhere | | | |
| Total | 0 | 0 | |
| SUB-TOTAL your income needs | | | |

## Expenditure for children living with you or that you pay for

| Item | Current cost per month | Estimated future cost per month |
|---|---|---|
| **SECTION 12: Education for children** | | |
| School fees | | |
| Child maintenance | | |
| University fees | | |
| Fares/travel to school/college | | |
| Extras on the school bill | | |
| School meals | | |
| Uniform and special clothing, e.g. sports | | |
| Extra tuition | | |
| Sports and other equipment, e.g. books | | |
| Dancing lessons | | |
| Clothing and footwear for dancing | | |
| Music lessons | | |
| Cost of musical instrument | | |
| Swimming lessons | | |
| Drama lessons | | |
| School photographs | | |
| Other – specify | | |
| Total | 0 | 0 |
| **SECTION 13: Clothing and footwear for children** | | |
| Clothes | | |
| Sports clothes | | |
| Footwear | | |
| Sports footwear | | |
| Coats | | |
| Accessories | | |
| Other – specify | | |
| Total | 0 | 0 |
| **SECTION 14: Activities, holidays for children** | | |
| Sports and other equipment | | |
| Sports club membership | | |
| Cubs/Scouts/Brownies/Guides | | |

| Item | Current cost per month | Estimated future cost per month |
|---|---|---|
| Trips/activities | | |
| Toys/equipment | | |
| Books/CDs/DVDs | | |
| Computer games | | |
| Hobby equipment, e.g. paints, golf clubs | | |
| Cinema/theatre/pop concerts/festivals | | |
| Museums/exhibitions/fairs | | |
| School trips | | |
| Other – specify | | |
| Total | 0 | 0 |
| **SECTION 15: Miscellaneous for children** | | |
| Baby requisites, nappies toiletries, etc. | | |
| Dentist/hygienist | | |
| Optician | | |
| Medical expenses | | |
| Chemist/pharmaceutical expenses | | |
| Mobile telephone | | |
| Toiletries/make-up | | |
| Hairdressing | | |
| Laundry, dry cleaning, shoe repairs, etc. | | |
| Travel expenses | | |
| Birthday parties | | |
| Christmas/birthday/other presents | | |
| Presents for friends/other family members | | |
| Children's pocket money | | |
| Other – specify | | |
| Total | 0 | 0 |
| SUB-TOTAL income needs for children | 0 | 0 |

| Summary | | |
|---|---|---|
| Housing – main home | 0 | 0 |
| Housing – second/other property | 0 | 0 |
| Food and household | 0 | 0 |
| Clothes, footwear, etc. | 0 | 0 |
| Other expenses | 0 | 0 |
| Help in the house | 0 | 0 |
| Car and other transport | 0 | 0 |
| Personal expenditure | 0 | 0 |
| Entertainment, hobbies, holidays | 0 | 0 |
| Insurance and savings | 0 | 0 |
| Employment expenses | 0 | 0 |
| Miscellaneous | 0 | 0 |
| For the children | 0 | 0 |
| Total | 0 | 0 |

# Annex 3D

## Letter to client explaining disclosure requirements, self-help and online protection

Dear [*name of client*]

As you are aware, it is important that both you and [*name of spouse*] provide full frank and clear financial information about your individual and joint circumstances. This obligation is often referred to as 'disclosure'. You need to provide ongoing information, as it happens, about your personal and financial circumstances, as these will have an impact on any settlement prospects and court proceedings.

The duty to provide disclosure is owed to your spouse but principally to the court. If you are not sure whether to tell me about a change in your circumstances then you should err on the side of safety and let me know.

### Failure to give full disclosure

If you do not give me information which is later found out, it is possible that any order made will be set aside. This means that you may need to go through the financial disclosure process again and a different order could be made. This can lead to a duplication in legal costs and costs orders could be made against you. It is also possible that you will lose credibility if it is discovered that you have failed to give full and frank disclosure.

### Accessing your spouse's documents

There is often a concern that your spouse will not be as open and honest as you will be in these proceedings. This concern might possibly tempt you to help yourself to [*name of spouse*]'s documents. The courts are very strict about accessing documents that do not belong to you. **Please do not access or give me any documents that belong to [*name of spouse*].** If you access and give me [*name of spouse*]'s documents when you should not have done, I may not be able to represent you any further in these proceedings and the court might impose strict penalties on you for doing so.

If [*name of spouse*] has shared financial information and documentation with you in the past and you still have access to that information now, you may be able to obtain copies of the documents and share them with me. However, if you know that [*name of spouse*] would not want you to have those documents, you should not give me copies of them.

You should not access any of [*name of spouse*]'s personal communications at all. For example, this would include personal letters or emails from friends or family members.

## Online protection

I am aware that couples often share passwords and documents electronically with each other. I recommend that you change all of your passwords immediately.

I also recommend that you sever any iCloud accounts or cloud-based software that is connected to any devices held by your spouse. It is sometimes easy to forget that any documents you save on your laptop might also be uploading to your spouse's mobile devices. I therefore recommend that you carry out a thorough check of your online activity to ensure that your spouse has no access.

Likewise, you should not access [*name of spouse*]'s documents or online activity that you may legitimately have had access to in the past. This means that even if they forget to change their passwords or accidently leave you with access to their documents, you should not access them. You should be aware that, if you were to illegally access [*name of spouse*]'s documents on their computer, criminal sanctions could be imposed upon you.

If you think that [*name of spouse*] will destroy documents as a result of these proceedings we could apply to the court to stop [him/her] from doing so. Please discuss this issue with me if you think that important documents are going to be destroyed and I can advise you further.

If you have information belonging to [*name of spouse*] that you think is important, please speak to me about this first **without** sending me the documents.

# Annex 3E

## Letter enclosing other party's Form E and next steps

Dear [*name of client*]

I am pleased to confirm that I have received [*name of spouse*]'s financial statement and documents. I enclose a copy of it for your attention. These documents are confidential and you must not show them to anyone other than your professional financial adviser or your accountant.

You might find it daunting to look through the statement and the documents attached but I would ask that you read everything carefully. I will be going through the financial statement myself so that I can prepare documents to file with the Court before the hearing on [*date*].

The Court will allow us to ask questions about [*name of spouse*]'s financial disclosure before the hearing. We are permitted to ask [him/her]:

1. to clarify any matters in the statement;
2. to identify any unusual transactions in their bank or credit statements;
3. to ask about assets that we think might be missing.

I would therefore like you to look through the financial statement and documents to identify any of the following:

1. Unusual bank transactions. These might be payments to someone you don't recognise, recurring direct debit payments, credits from sources you don't recognise or transfers to accounts you don't recognise.
2. Assets that you think are missing from the disclosure. This may be a personal possession such as a car or jewellery, or it might be an investment that used to exist but that doesn't appear in the financial statement.
3. Anything in the statement that you think is untrue or incorrect.
4. Anything in the financial statement or supporting documents that you would like more information about.

### Questionnaire

I will then prepare a document called a request for further information and documentation, also known as 'the questionnaire'. I will send you this document in a draft format so that you can see which documents we are asking [*name of spouse*] to produce and the questions we are asking [him/her] to answer.

The Judge at the First Appointment will decide whether we are allowed to receive the information we want from [*name of spouse*].

We are not likely to get another opportunity to ask [*name of spouse*] questions until the final hearing and so we should make sure we ask any relevant questions now.

### *Documents to be prepared for the court hearing*

There are documents that I need to prepare in advance of the hearing. The purpose of these documents is to put the case information in a collated, short format to help the busy judge. I will be working on these and sharing them with you.

### *First Appointment*

As you know, we need to attend the First Appointment on [*date of hearing*]. I will write to you before the hearing to let you know what to expect. For the time being, I am preparing the paperwork to submit on [*date*].

Please contact me to give me your views on [*name of spouse*]'s disclosure so that I can start to draft the above paperwork.

# Annex 3F

## Soft loans and how they are treated by the court

The court will be concerned with the parties' net assets, and therefore any liabilities must be evidenced and taken into account. The court may draw a distinction between a **soft loan** and a **hard loan**. A hard loan is one that will generally be regarded as repayable.

The definition and treatment of a soft loan is not specifically dealt with in legislation, and the approach in case law is often fact-specific and therefore to a degree inconsistent.

However, useful guidance was provided in the case of *P* v. *Q (financial remedies)* by HHJ Hess, who said that, as a matter of general principle, for an advance of money to be considered to be a gift as opposed to a loan, there must be evidence of an intention to give. Further, that in the family court, the inclusion or exclusion of a technically enforceable debt in an asset schedule can depend on its softness/hardness, which is 'an elusive topic to nail down'. He went on to consider case law and derived the following summary of principles:

- Once a judge has decided that a contractually binding obligation by a party to the marriage towards a third party exists, the court may properly go on to consider whether the obligation is a hard obligation or loan, in which case it should appear on the judges' computation table, or is in the category of a soft obligation or loan, in which case the judge may decide as an exercise of discretion to leave it out of the computation table.
- There is no hard or fast test as to when an obligation or loan will fall into one category or another and case law reveals a wide variety of circumstances which can cause a particular obligation or loan to fall on one side or other of the line, but a common feature is whether or not it is likely in reality that the obligation will be enforced.
- Factors which may on their own, or in combination, point the judge towards the conclusion that an obligation is in the category of a *hard* obligation include that:
  - it is an obligation to a finance company;
  - the terms of the obligation have 'the feel' of a normal commercial arrangement;
  - the obligation arises out of a written agreement;
  - there is a written demand for payment, a threat of or actual litigation or actual or consequent intervention in the financial remedies proceedings;
  - there has not been a delay in enforcing the obligation; and
  - the amount of money is such that it would be less likely for a creditor to be likely to waive the obligation either wholly or partly.
- Factors which may on their own, or in combination, point the judge towards the conclusion that an obligation is in the category of a *soft* obligation include that:
  - it is an obligation to a friend or family member with whom the debtor remains on good terms and who is unlikely to want the debtor to suffer hardship;

- the obligation arose informally and the terms of the obligation do not have the feel of a normal commercial arrangement;
- there has been no written demand for payment despite the due date having passed;
- there has been a delay in enforcing the obligation; and
- the amount of money is such that it would be more likely for the creditor to waive the obligation, either wholly or partly, albeit that the amount of money involved is not necessarily decisive and there are examples in authorities of large amounts of money being treated as being soft obligations.

Further examples of cases where the court considered obligations and loans include:

- The case of *M* v. *M (Financial Remedies)*, where the wife's loans from her family were described as being 'personal to her and not jointly owed with the husband'. As there was no suggestion that repayment of the monies was being demanded, there were no loan agreements and the wife's family had shown considerable willingness to assist her financially, these fell to be treated as soft loans, but although the court was entitled to take account of the willingness of family members to make funds available by gift or loan, the court's function was to distribute the resources of the parties, not the resources of their wider families.
- *TT* v. *CDS (Financial Remedies)*, where the husband's inability to provide evidence of his indebtedness, including loans from friends and relatives totalling £865,000, was described as 'astonishing' and various liabilities were excluded by the court.
- *ABX* v. *SBX (DX intervening)*, where a family loan was documented in a loan agreement and formed part of the declaration of trust in respect of the matrimonial home, Francis J accepted that the loan would be termed 'soft', but that it would be treated 'as a genuine obligation'.
- *B* v. *S (financial remedy: marital property regime)*, where the judge considered a family loan in that case 'as being notionally payable out of non-matrimonial assets, if they ever are in fact repaid, which I doubt'.
- *A* v. *A*, where family loans were taken into account but to varying degrees based on the history of repayment and the facts of that case.
- *M* v. *B (ancillary proceedings: lump sum)*, where Thorpe LJ highlighted the importance of the distinction between hard and soft loans and said, 'In all these cases it is one of the paramount considerations, in applying the [legal criteria], to endeavour to stretch what is available to cover the need of each for a home, particularly where there are young children involved'.
- *H* v. *H*, where Baron J said of funds advanced to the husband by his parents, 'The monies may well be termed "a loan", but of the very softest kind. Thus, I do not propose to regard any such loan as a real liability in this case'.
- In *R* v. *K (Financial Remedies: Conduct)*, the court was concerned with whether the husband and his business associates had fabricated or exaggerated liabilities, and was particularly critical of both the quality of the evidence and the absence of documentary evidence. Baker J found that the husband had been 'unable to provide a coherent account'.
- In *Kliers* v. *Kliers*, the parties had liabilities in relation to council tax and HMRC repayments (in relation to which there were issues of illegality). Although the

> wife argued that as the husband had been able to borrow funds within his community to repay some of the liabilities, she should be entitled to the benefit of those repayments, the court concluded that it was fair in all the circumstances to treat the debts which accrued during the marriage as being joint debts that should be taken from the marital assets before division.

As you can see from the examples given, how debt is treated depends on the circumstances of the case in terms of what assets there are and how the debt arose and to whom the debt is payable. In some cases, the assets are not enough to go around and the court will nearly always put the meeting of basic 'need' above repaying debt, whether hard or soft. Most often, soft debts are not taken into account. Of course, you can agree as part of your settlement that certain debts will be repaid; however, if the court is making the decision, the court may not take the same view. It is also important to note that the court cannot order one party to make a payment to a third party who is not part of the court proceedings. For example, a husband or wife cannot be ordered to pay £XX to Aunty Mabel to satisfy a debt.

# Annex 3G

## Financial applications: pre-application protocol[1,2]

### Summary of the Pre-application Protocol for financial remedy proceedings

1. The Protocol sets out the key steps the court will expect parties to take in relation to non-court dispute resolution (NCDR), i.e. resolving a dispute other than through the court process, before starting court proceedings. The Protocol also underlines the duty to make full and honest disclosure. The full Protocol is attached to this document. Everyone is required to comply with the terms of the Protocol, even if they have not had professional advice from a legal representative.
2. Before coming to court, unless there are safety concerns or other good reasons not to do so, the court will expect parties to have attended at least one form of NCDR. Please see paragraphs 10, 11, and 12 of the Protocol for more details.
3. All applicants are required to attend a MIAM before they start court proceedings unless they have a valid exemption, and all respondents are expected to do so. An authorised mediator will give the parties information about which form of NCDR may be most suitable.
4. If court proceedings are started, a party must set out their position on using NCDR using **Form FM5** (which can be accessed here [**https://assets.publishing.service.gov.uk/media/662fafc68cf6065df2e3cba4/FM5_0424.pdf**]) and send this to the Court and to the other party at least 7 working days before the first hearing or as directed by the court.
5. If the parties have not attended a form of NCDR, the court may decline to commence the court timetable or suspend the court timetable so that the parties may attend a form of NCDR. The court will also take into account any failure by a party to attend a MIAM or form of NCDR when considering the question of costs (together with any other failure to comply with the Protocol, see paragraph 25) and may make an order requiring that party to pay the other party's costs.
6. Lengthy and unnecessary correspondence must be avoided and the parties must seek to identify the issues as soon as possible. The impact of any correspondence upon the reader must always be considered, particularly the first letter.
7. Before starting court proceedings, the parties should attempt, where possible, voluntary financial disclosure and negotiation. Any disclosure must be full, honest and open. Parties must be advised of this duty by their legal advisers, including the ongoing duty to disclose any material changes. Requests for disclosure must be necessary, relevant and limited to what is reasonably required.
8. Pre-application disclosure should be provided using **Form E** (financial remedy proceedings) which can be accessed here [**https://assets.publishing.service.gov.**

1.  Annex to Family Procedure Rules 2010, Practice Direction 9A – Application for a Financial Remedy, last updated 24 May 2024. Available at **www.justice.gov.uk/documents/fpr-pd-update-no-5-of-2024.pdf**
2. Extracted to give to clients.

**uk/media/63c132468fa8f516ac0d5a6d/Form_E_0123_save.pdf]**; Form E1 (financial claims for the benefit of children under Schedule 1 of the Children Act 1989) which can be accessed here [**https://assets.publishing.service.gov.uk/media/661910c5679e9c8d921dfe4a/Form_E1_0424.pdf**] or Form E2 (application to vary an existing order other than to capitalise periodical payments) which can be accessed here [**https://assets.publishing.service.gov.uk/media/6515c07a6dfda600148e3846/Form_E2_0123.pdf**]. Financial information can be summarised in Template ES2 which can be accessed here [**www.judiciary.uk/guidance-and-resources/notice-from-the-financial-remedies-court-4**].

The Protocol helpfully signposts a number of on-line resources for the parties to consider to help them resolve the dispute without the need for court proceedings (paragraph 40).

## Pre-application Protocol: financial remedy proceedings

### *Introduction*

1. Pre-application protocols explain the conduct and set out the steps the court expects parties to take before starting court proceedings.
2. This Protocol applies to all applications for a financial remedy as defined by rule 2.3. It covers all classes of case, including applications for periodical payments, lump sum, property adjustment and/or pension sharing orders. It applies whatever the size of the parties' assets and whether it is a so-called "needs" or "sharing" case. It applies whether the parties are legally represented or not.
3. This Protocol underlines the duty of parties to make full and honest disclosure of all material facts, documents, and other information relevant to the issues.
4. Any legal representatives instructed should give a copy of this Protocol to all parties, and explain its meaning and implications to their client, before they start court proceedings.

### *Objectives*

5. The objectives of this Protocol are to encourage appropriate engagement in non-court dispute resolution and to:
   (a) enable the parties to understand each other's position;
   (b) assist the parties in deciding how to proceed;
   (c) identify the issues in dispute;
   (d) narrow the scope of the dispute;
   (e) try to settle the issues without court proceedings;
   (f) support efficient management of dispute resolution; and
   (g) reduce the costs of resolving the dispute.

## *Compliance*

6. To comply with this Protocol the court will usually expect the parties to have done the following:

   (a) attended a MIAM with an authorised mediator, unless a valid exemption applies;
   (b) considered, and unless there is good reason for not doing, proposed and engaged in appropriate non-court dispute resolution;
   (c) provided full disclosure (information relevant to the issues in dispute) to the other party, including appropriate financial disclosure;
   (d) clearly set out their position (including the orders they would wish the court to make were proceedings started); and
   (e) attempted negotiation (trying to agree the issues in dispute) by making reasonable proposals for settlement.

## *Attendance at a Mediation Information and Assessment Meeting (MIAM)*

7. A MIAM is a meeting where an authorised mediator will give the parties information about non-court dispute resolution, explain its benefits, and indicate which method(s) of non-court dispute resolution may be most suitable.
8. All prospective applicants are required to attend a MIAM before they start court proceedings unless they have a valid exemption. All prospective respondents are expected to attend a MIAM before proceedings are started, unless there is a good reason why they should not do so.
9. The list of exemptions for attending a MIAM are set out at rule 3.8. A link to the list of exemptions can be found here: **www.justice.gov.uk/courts/procedure-rules/family/parts/part_03#para3.8.**

## *Non-court dispute resolution*

10. Non-court dispute resolution is defined in rule 2.3. It means methods of resolving a dispute other than through the court process and includes, but is not limited to, the following:

    (a) mediation (a third party seeking to facilitate a resolution);
    (b) arbitration (a third party deciding the dispute);
    (c) neutral evaluation (a third party giving a neutral indication on the dispute, such as a private Financial Dispute Resolution process); and
    (d) the collaborative process (the parties and their collaboratively trained legal representatives meeting together, but with those legal representatives being prevented from representing the parties in later court proceedings if the collaborative process does not result in settlement).

11. The court may also consider the parties having obtained legal advice via the "single lawyer" or a "one couple, one lawyer" scheme as good evidence of a constructive attempt to obtain advice and avoid unnecessary proceedings, if they have complied with paragraph 6 above.

12. Although there is a place for constructive negotiation via correspondence between legal representatives, that alone shall not be a sufficient attempt at non-court dispute resolution for the purposes of this Protocol. Other forms of negotiation between legal representatives, such as round-table meetings, may be considered sufficient depending on when and how they took place.
13. All parties and legal representatives should seek, from the outset, to engage in appropriate non-court dispute resolution, and keep any initial decision not to do so under careful ongoing review.
14. Before starting court proceedings, the court will expect parties to have attended at least one form of non-court dispute resolution, unless there are safety concerns or there is another good reason not to do so.
15. Legal representatives should make the parties aware that if they have not attempted at least one form of non-court dispute resolution before starting court proceedings then the court (on being informed by a party that this is the case or by the court finding out of its own initiative) may (i) decline to commence the court timetable by the issue of a Form C (Notice of a First Appointment); or (ii) suspend the same and instead make such directions as it thinks appropriate to ensure that at least one form of non-court dispute resolution has been attempted before directions on Form C are given.
16. If one party is not willing to attend non-court dispute resolution, they should give reasons in writing so that (i) the other party is clear about their position and the reasons given for it; and (ii) if court proceedings are started the position is clear to the court when it is considering whether, and if so how, to encourage non-court dispute resolution.
17. Before starting court proceedings, parties should bear in mind the following:
    (a) although there may be an advantage in having a court timetable, many (if not all) of the same benefits can be achieved within a non-court dispute resolution process such as arbitration where the parties agree that the arbitrator's case management powers are to be similar to those available to a court;
    (b) if court proceedings are issued, the court will have the possibility of non-court dispute resolution forefront in its mind:
        (i) by rule 1.4, the court must further the overriding objective by actively managing cases. By rule 1.2(2)(f), active case management includes encouraging the parties to use non-court dispute resolution if the court considers that appropriate and facilitating the use of such procedure;
        (ii) by rule 3.3(1), the court must consider, at every stage in proceedings, whether non-court dispute resolution is appropriate;
        (iii) by rule 3.3(1A), before a first hearing, and before any later hearing when the court so requires, a party must file with the court and serve on all other parties a form (Form FM5) setting out their views on using non-court dispute resolution as a means of resolving the matters raised in the proceedings. By paragraph 10C of PD3A, unless the court directs otherwise, the form is to be filed and served seven days before the relevant hearing;
        (iv) by rule 3.4(1A), where the timetabling of proceedings allows sufficient time for these steps to be taken, the court should encourage parties, as

it considers appropriate, to obtain information and advice about, consider using and undertake non-court dispute resolution; and

(v) by rule 28.3(7), a failure, without good reason, to attend non-court dispute resolution is an express reason for the court to consider departing from the general rule of no order as to costs.

18. If court proceedings are started, the parties may be required by the court to provide evidence that non-court dispute resolution has been attempted or that there are good reasons for it not having been attempted.
19. If the parties are engaged in non-court dispute resolution, an application to the court should not be made until the process has concluded, unless there are good reasons, which could include, but would not be limited to, seeking orders from the court to prevent assets from being disposed of or dissipated.
20. Although there may be good reasons (for example, where there is a real risk one party may start competing proceedings in another jurisdiction or dissipate assets) to start court proceedings before attempting non-court dispute resolution, the court will still expect parties to attempt non-court dispute resolution to resolve other issues in dispute once the urgent issue which caused the party to start court proceedings has been resolved.

### *General principles*

21. Parties and legal representatives must always bear in mind the court's overriding objective as set out at rule 1.1 to resolve cases justly, as quickly and fairly as possible, in ways that are proportionate to the nature, importance and complexity of the issues, and without costs being unreasonably incurred. By rule 1.3 the parties are required to help the court further the overriding objective. These obligations apply equally to conduct before as well as after proceedings have started.
22. The needs of any children should be addressed and safeguarded.
23. The procedures which it is appropriate to follow should be conducted with minimum distress to the parties and in a manner designed to promote as good a continuing relationship between the parties and any children affected as is possible in the circumstances.
24. It is not acceptable for the costs of any case to be disproportionate to the financial value of the subject matter of the dispute. The principle of proportionality must therefore always be borne in mind. Proportionality is a factor the court will take into account when considering whether, and if so to what extent, to make an order for one party to pay the costs of the other party.
25. Parties and legal representatives should be aware that where a court is considering whether to make an order requiring one party to pay the costs of another party, it will take into account (i) any open pre-application offers to settle; (ii) if a party did not attend a MIAM and was not exempt from doing so; (iii) the FM5; (iv) whether a party has provided appropriate financial disclosure and, if so, when; and (v) a failure, without good reason, to attend non-court dispute resolution or a premature and unjustified abandonment of ongoing non-court dispute resolution.

## Correspondence

26. All correspondence must focus on the clarification of claims and identification of issues and their resolution. Parties and legal representatives will usually be expected to raise and recommend non-court dispute resolution in early correspondence. Protracted and unnecessary correspondence must be avoided.
27. The impact of any correspondence (including the time at which it is sent) upon the reader must always be considered. Any correspondence which raises irrelevant issues, or which might cause the other party to adopt an entrenched, polarised, or hostile position is to be discouraged.
28. The circumstances of parties to an application for a financial remedy are so various that it would be difficult to prepare a specimen first letter. However, the tone and content of the initial letter is important and the guidelines in paragraphs 26 and 27 should be followed. Where a first letter is drafted by a legal representative, it should be approved in advance by the client. Particular consideration should be given as to how the first letter will be received by the person to whom it is sent, having regard to its tone and content.
29. Legal representatives writing to an unrepresented party should always recommend that he or she seeks independent legal advice and, if sent in hard copy, enclose a second copy of the letter to be passed to any legal representative instructed. A reasonable time limit for an answer may be 14 days.

## Identifying the issues

30. Parties must seek to clarify their claims and identify the issues between them as soon as possible.

## Disclosure and negotiation

31. Before starting court proceedings, parties and their legal representatives (or those facilitating non-court dispute resolution) should consider whether the case is suitable for pre-application financial disclosure and negotiation. This option may be particularly suitable where providing or obtaining financial disclosure is not likely to be an issue or has already been adequately dealt with separately.
32. If the parties give pre-application financial disclosure, they must provide full and honest disclosure to the other party of facts, information and documents which are material and sufficiently accurate and up-to-date to enable proper negotiations then to take place. Openness in all dealings is essential.
33. Legal representatives must tell their clients in clear terms of this duty and of the possible consequences of providing false information without an honest belief in its truth.
34. The duty of disclosure is an ongoing obligation until a final financial remedies order has been made and therefore includes the duty to disclose any material changes after initial disclosure has been given. Any agreement reached by the parties which is based on dishonest information supplied in pre-application disclosure is very unlikely to be upheld by the court. Legal representatives are

referred to Resolution's Good Practice Guides at **https://resolution.org.uk/membership/our-code-of-practice/good-practice-guides**. They can also contact The Law Society Practice Advice Service on 020 7320 5685 or practiceadvice@lawsociety.org.uk.

35. If parties provide financial disclosure before starting proceedings, they should do so using the appropriate financial statement (Form E, E1 or E2) as a guide to the format. The three forms used in financial remedy proceedings are as follows:
    (a) Form E (which is used to give financial disclosure when resolving financial claims on divorce or dissolution of civil partnership): **https://assets.publishing.service.gov.uk/media/63c132468fa8f516ac0d5a6d/Form_E_0123_save.pdf.**
    (b) Form E1 (which is used to give financial disclosure when resolving financial claims for the benefit of children): **https://assets.publishing.service.gov.uk/media/661910c5679e9c8d921dfe4a/Form_E1_0424.pdf.**
    (c) Form E2 (which is used to give financial disclosure when resolving financial claims on an application to vary an existing order other than to capitalise an order for periodical payments): **https://assets.publishing.service.gov.uk/media/6515c07a6dfda600148e3846/Form_E2_0123.pdf.**
36. The financial information can then be summarised in Template ES2 (Composite asset and income schedule): **www.judiciary.uk/guidance-and-resources/notice-from-the-financial-remedies-court-4**.
37. If the appropriate statement is the Form E1 or E2 the parties may, by agreement and where appropriate, use the Form E which requires more extensive and detailed financial information than the other two forms.
38. Documents should only be disclosed to the extent they are required by the financial statement in the first instance. Any requests for further disclosure should be limited to seeking information and documentation that is necessary, relevant, and proportionate. Excessive or disproportionate costs should not be incurred.
39. In the event of pre-application disclosure and negotiation, a court application should not be made when a settlement is a reasonable prospect.

## *Other resources*

40. Legal representatives are encouraged to inform their clients of resources which may help them resolve the dispute without the need for court proceedings, and unrepresented parties are encouraged to consider such resources. These include but are not limited to:
    (a) LawforLife's 'Advicenow' guides: **www.advicenow.org.uk/affordable-advice-help-family-problems**;
    (b) Family Justice Council's 'Sorting out Finances on Divorce' (Second Edition, March 2024): **www.judiciary.uk/wp-content/uploads/2023/06/1.-Sorting-Out-Finances-on-Divorce-2024.final-for-publication.pdf**; and
    (c) Pension Advisory Group's 'A Guide to the Treatment of Pensions on Divorce' (Second Edition, January 2024): **www.nuffieldfoundation.org/wp-content/uploads/2023/A-guide-to-the-treatment-of-pensions-on-divorce-2nd-edition.pdf.**

## *Summary*

41. The aim of all steps that are taken before the start of court proceedings must be to assist the parties to resolve their differences speedily and fairly or at least narrow the issues and, should that not be possible, to assist the court to do so.

# 4 First directions appointment

## 4.1 Introduction and preparation steps

The precedents in this chapter are designed to deal with all matters up to and including the first directions appointment (the 'First Appointment' or 'FDA'). The First Appointment is usually the point in time when the court will appoint experts if a proper application has been made in accordance with FPR 2010, Part 25. The court will also record any points of agreement and give permission to raise a questionnaire with the corresponding direction to reply, after it has considered the questions within each questionnaire. Bear in mind that while this may be your 'day to day', for your client this will be probably be the first time they are dealing with this type of application. You must explain all the steps and documentation to your client.

When the Form E has been exchanged with the other party, you should send a copy to your client but you need to explain to your client what you want them to do with it and what you want back from them. When you send the draft questionnaire to them, be careful in your explanation of the purpose of the questionnaire and the limitations of it.

You should be fully familiar with the Efficiency Statement and the requirements within that.

In short, in the run up to the First Appointment, you will have a number of things to do:

- Send the Form E and documents of the other party to your client. You need to know if they have any comments and if they think anything is missing.
- Draft a questionnaire to be approved by the court. This has to be sent to your client and explained to them before you file and serve it.
- Critically consider the questionnaire you receive from the other party, in the context of the case and the relevant issues.
- Prepare the Form H statement of costs. Again, this must be sent to your client and explained to them before you file and serve it. This is a good point at which to consider whether your costs estimate needs to be revised.
- Prepare the Form ES1 and Form ES2 or respond to it. Again, this has to be done with the input of your client.
- Prepare, file and serve Form G.
- Prepare, file and serve Form FM5 regarding your client's position in respect of non-court dispute resolution.
- Consider, together with the solicitor for the other party, whether a joint mortgage capacity can be obtained and if not, you need obtain this for your client or ask your client to obtain it for themselves. It is an indication at this

stage, which is needed to comply with the Efficiency Statement, and not a full report.

- Ask your client to send you particulars of properties that they consider suitable for themselves and particulars of properties they consider suitable for the other party. Guide your client in this. Remind them to ensure that there is parity of property quality – no castles for one and hovels for the other; that if they have children, it will need to be suitable for the children, who will be there some of the time; and that it is realistic within the budget for each of them. 'Premium' areas should be avoided if the finances will not stretch to it.
- Consider with your client what aspects can be agreed. Can you agree the value of the former family home for FDR/negotiation purposes? Do you agree that a particular expert is needed and why? Your focus should be on attempting to resolve the issues between the parties, not merely going through the motions.
- Identify the directions the court needs to be asked to consider.
- Prepare, file and serve an application pursuant to Part 25 if you consider that an expert is required. This often requires quotes to be obtained and a draft letter of instruction to be written. Do not leave this until the last moment or expect to be able to make an oral application at the First Appointment. You must comply with FPR 2010, rule 25.6(d), which provides that an application for expert evidence should be made no later than the First Appointment.
- Prepare or consider the hearing bundle to be used at the hearing. You should be fully conversant with FPR 2010, Practice Direction 27A and also President's Memorandum: Guidance on E-Bundles for Use in the Family Court and Family Division issued 18 February 2022.
- When uploading the documents to the digital portal, you should be fully conversant with the HMCTS guidance on use of the portal, and remember to share documents with the other party. It is important to keep up to date with judicial guidance and HMCTS guidance, which are regularly updated.

## 4.2 Choice of advocate

Prior to the First Appointment, clients should be able to choose the person they would like to represent them at the hearing. It may be that you do not undertake advocacy but there is another person within the firm who is able to take this on, rather than engaging counsel. **Annex 4C** offers a number of choices:

1. You undertake the advocacy yourself at your usual hourly rate.
2. Another person within the firm undertakes advocacy at their usual hourly rate.
3. A barrister is instructed to deal with the case on a fixed fee.
4. Additionally, it is possible that a junior from the firm may be sent to the hearing to assist the barrister and their costs also charged to the client.

You should ensure that advocacy fees are paid in advance, particularly where a barrister is instructed. It is a point of conduction for a solicitor that when the brief is delivered to counsel, the solicitor is liable for counsel's fee. It should also be noted that when a brief is delivered to counsel, the conduct of the matter passes to counsel, so any major decisions should be made in concert with counsel.

It is ordinary practice for family barristers to charge a 'deemed fee' for abortive preparation work and for possibly turning away other work due to the scheduled hearing. This means that if the case settles before the hearing or is taken out of the list by the court the barrister will be able to charge all or part of their fee. Counsel's clerk will usually inform you of any deemed fee arrangements when counsel is booked; however, it is good practice to check the deemed fee dates and diarise them. Remember also to advise your client of this practice, particularly given the issues with listing at the time of writing (August 2024).

It is also worth explaining to the client the rules around who will be responsible for preparing bundles, particularly if the applicant is a litigant in person and this responsibility falls upon the respondent. FPR 2010, Practice Direction 27A sets out the rules for bundle preparation. The Family Procedure Rules Committee has issued a consultation regarding possible amendment of PD27A to take account of the Efficiency Statement and the President's guidance on electronic bundling (see **3.7**).

If the other party is a litigant in person, the client should be told that the client may not have a legal representative at the hearing. Instead, clients may ask for a friend to accompany them to the hearing. Usually no formal applications are made before the hearing but such a request will often be made at the hearing. The Law Society's practice note on dealing with litigants in person contains invaluable information for practitioners (**www.lawsociety.org.uk/topics/civil-litigation/litigants-in-person-guidelines-for-lawyers**).

## 4.3 Form H Estimate of costs (financial remedy)

Form H Estimate of costs (financial remedy) is available online at **www.gov.uk/government/publications/form-h-estimate-of-costs-financial-remedy**. It is very straightforward and needs to be filed by each party at the First Appointment (FPR 2010, rule 9.27). It is interesting to note that there is no specific requirement that each party must exchange their costs estimate with the other party, only that they produce the costs estimate at the hearing. Although it is commonplace for parties to exchange estimates of costs with each other when filing questionnaires and statements of issues, there is no procedural rule that requires this to take place. The Form H has to be uploaded to the portal prior to the First Appointment and the costs stated will be recorded in the directions order made at the First Appointment.

The form is easy to follow. You will benefit from ensuring that invoices are raised to your client:

- upon issue of the Form A to demark the costs incurred prior to the Form A being issued;
- prior to the First Appointment to aid calculation of figures for the Form H;
- after the First Appointment to aid later calculation of figures for the FDR; and
- after the FDR to aid calculation of figures in contemplation of a final hearing.

The Form H has a front 'summary' sheet with sections clearly marked for costs incurred at each stage of the application. For privately paying clients, the costs figures are entered into the 'indemnity rates' column. Note that the Form H is verified by a statement of truth. You can sign this but only after having sent and explained the Form H to your client. Either you or the client need to sign the form; not both.

## 4.4 Statement of costs (summary assessment)

FPR 2010, Practice Direction 28A states at para.4.5 that if a party seeks a costs order against another party, this should be made plain in open correspondence or in skeleton arguments before the date of the hearing. Where a summary assessment of costs is appropriate the parties should file a statement of costs using Form N260. This is rarely used in financial cases.

Form N260 is available online. This form must be completed and served on the other party no less than 24 hours before the date of the hearing. The form must be signed by a partner at the firm of solicitors, or a director of an LLP.

On the first page, your details should be inserted. These should include your level of qualification/training and the associated grade derived from that. The box at the end of page 3 sets out the various grades and levels of qualification.

The form should be completed to indicate your attendances on the client, experts, counsel, court and any other party. An estimate of the time spent attending the hearing should be inserted if a representative from the firm is attending; otherwise, counsel's fees can be inserted at page 4.

Any other expenses such as the initial court fee and any disbursements incurred at the Land Registry or elsewhere should be inserted under the heading 'other expenses'. The correct rate of VAT should be applied and a grand total of all costs should appear on page 4. The grand total should not exceed the maximum sum of costs chargeable to the client: this is known as the indemnity principle.

## 4.5 Post-hearing action

It is the responsibility of the applicant's representative (or the respondent's representative if the applicant is a litigant in person) to draft the order for the court to approve. The Standard Order template should be used. These can be downloaded from the judiciary website. They are the suite of template orders approved by the lead financial remedies judge for England and Wales to be used in financial remedy matters. The draft order, when agreed between the parties, is uploaded to the digital portal for approval.

The draft order should be sent to the client with a simple explanation and timeline plan of action. You will receive an email notification of when the order has been sealed and is available for download from the portal. This can take some time if a listing date is required for FDR. You should diarise and keep this under review.

Similarly, you should diarise each action step according to the order made at First Appointment.

## 4.6 Instructing an expert

### *4.6.1 What experts?*

The experts most usually instructed in financial applications, in order of frequency, are:

- estate agents;
- surveyors;
- pension experts;
- accountants;
- mortgage consultants;
- GPs or other medical professionals;
- business valuers;
- forensic accountants.

#### Estate agents (letter of instruction: Annex 4E)

For the majority of cases, particularly needs based cases, the person the court will nominate to value a property will be an estate agent. A common method is for one party to nominate five agents, the other party to select three of the agents and then the three chosen are asked to appraise the property to give a value likely to be achieved on exchange of contracts. This is not the same as the marketing value, which is generally higher to allow for some negotiation room. Of the three valuations given, either the average will be taken or the median. Make sure you know which you think is best.

Estate agents will need to know how to gain access to the property to view it and, if there is a lease, the remaining unexpired term of the lease plus any management fees payable by the leaseholder.

Estate agents generally do not charge a fee. Appointment of estate agents to appraise a property generally, in practice, would not warrant a formal application on a costs/practicality basis.

#### Surveyors

Surveyors are generally only used for more complex properties. Examples might be:

- An investment House in Multiple Occupation.
- Where there are interveners who have invested in the property and values are needed before and after the work funded by the investment was done.
- Where there are extensive repair works that one party says are necessary and the other says are not needed. A figure may be required for the repairs.
- Where there has been significant improvement work funded by one party from a non-matrimonial source/asset, unmatched by the other.

Surveyors will charge a fee. A surveyor is not a usual appointment and so an application will be needed if your client says that a surveyor, rather than estate agent, should be appointed.

## Pension experts

The family practitioner should familiarise themselves with the Pension Advisory Group report, 'A Guide to the Treatment of Pensions on Divorce' (Second Edition, 2024) for all matters concerning pensions, including the draft instruction letter to the expert. (The report is available from the Nuffield Foundation website, **www.nuffieldfoundation.org**.) The organisation Advicenow also has leaflets in plain language for a litigant in person that can be downloaded for your clients.

The pension expert will need to know whether they are being instructed to calculate income equality in retirement; if so, the expert also needs to know what the date of retirement will be. This can sometimes be a thorny issue during divorce, particularly if one party does not agree with the age at which the other wishes to retire. This can easily be resolved by both practitioners having a telephone conference with the expert to agree on the date to be used before submitting the letter of instruction, rather than inserting multiple dates of retirement as this will produce multiple calculations which will increase the cost of the report. Asking for a number of options to be considered will not always help to settle the case as the report will then contain too many permutations.

The expert may be asked to calculate an offsetting figure so that one party can retain equity in the matrimonial home (or other capital) rather than take equality of income through pension transfer. Finally, it may be that the expert is asked to calculate a pension share to ensure a projected income at a certain level at state retirement age.

In the instructions section, the pension expert may also be asked to exclude periods of premarital pension contributions and/or post-separation pension contributions.

Some pension experts require the parties themselves to obtain the information required from the pension expert; others will apply for it themselves. Most have an established way of working with authority letters for your clients to sign if needed.

## Accountants (letter of instruction: Annex 4F)

While you should familiarise yourself with the tax regimes, principally for income tax and CGT, solicitors should not give tax advice but defer to an accountant. The most common issues are around CGT for a second property. Changes to the Capital Gains Tax Act 1992 have amended the provisions when a party no longer resides in the former family home but you should be alive to this issue.

In this instance the expert needs to know:

- how much it cost to purchase the asset;
- how much the asset is worth now;
- when dealing with a home, whether this was the primary principal residence (PPR) for either of the parties, giving details of the periods during which that was the case;
- if one of the parties has left the matrimonial home, the date they vacated; if they have not purchased another property, whether they are going to lose their PPR relief and will need to pay CGT;

- any expensive works done to the property that could be deducted from a capital gain before the calculation of tax.

## Mortgage consultants

Virtually all clients will need this expert as the court will need to consider housing need. An application is generally not made for their appointment since the standard directions order provides for this.

## GP or other medical professionals

If your client's case is that their health condition impacts on their earning capacity, whether short term or longer term, you will need medical evidence to support this. You will need to make an application for this evidence.

## Business valuers and/or forensic accountants (letter of instruction: Annex 4G)

These experts are rarely appointed in 'needs based' cases because the asset value versus the cost of obtaining the report is rarely justified.

In the letter of instructions, contact details are provided so that the expert can contact the accountant for the business and other key administrative personnel to obtain the information needed for the report. The expert will also need some background information in respect of the business.

The expert is usually instructed to provide a value of the company and, if each party has a financial interest in the company, to determine the value of the parties' shares. Tax issues are very important, so the expert will need to calculate CGT and any tax relief available if one party were to sell their shares to the other party or back to the business. Finally, the matter of liquidity is very important to understand if the company is to be able to raise the finance to buy out shares or to release capital in the near future.

It may also be important to understand the maintainable future earnings for the party who intends to remain in the business.

When instructed to investigate, a business accountant will sometimes be called a 'forensic accountant' as the accountant is examining evidence.

Remember it is the court that controls the evidence. Sometimes, if both parties are agreed that an expert should be appointed, a formal application is not made but the court is asked, at the First Appointment, to permit the evidence to be adduced. The court can, however, refuse the request, even if both parties are agreed. Any expert evidence will be restricted to that which in the opinion of the court is necessary to assist the court to resolve the proceedings.

### 4.6.2 *The process for instructing an expert*

The standard order for directions at First Appointment sets out the process. Generally, one party drafts the letter, the other is to approve it, and then the first is to dispatch it, all timetabled with dates by which each step must be done.

When you are instructing an expert, the purpose of the letter of instruction is to tell the expert:

- The names of the parties and their solicitors.
- Whether there are court proceedings ongoing.
- What the court has ordered the expert to do (or what you want the expert to do), with any background information or documentation you think the expert might need for this.
- The date by when their report is to be produced.
- The expert is neutral, giving expert opinion evidence to the court.
- FPR 2010, Part 25 and practice directions need to be complied with. The report must be verified with a statement of truth. Also, the report should not be more than 40 pages in length.
- Communication should be with all parties simultaneously, and any clarification questions should be sent to both solicitors at the same time. The expert can ask the court for clarification (FPR 2010, rule 25.17) but commonly, the expert will ask the solicitors.
- Fees are to be agreed before work starts. The letter of instruction should include information on who will be responsible for paying these fees.
- Note that in the Pension Advisory Group report, 'A Guide to the Treatment of Pensions on Divorce' (Second Edition, 2024) there is a template letter for instructing a pension expert.

The court order will generally indicate how long each party has to raise questions to the expert (in default FPR 2010 state that the parties have 10 days from the report being filed to raise written questions), and who will pay the expert for the time taken in answering. If the order is silent, then the answers are treated as part of the report and the costs will be shared in the same way that the costs of the report are shared.

Responsibility for payment of the costs of the report should be set out in the order. In default, FPR 2010, rule 25.12(6) states that the parties are jointly and severally liable for the payment of the expert's fees and expenses. It is prudent therefore to ensure that the order states that the parties are each responsible for 50% of the costs. This is especially important when one of the parties is a litigant in person.

### 4.6.3 *What to do with the report*

You will need to send the report to your client as quickly as possible. In your letter to the client, you should explain the content of the report, any points you think need clarifying, any corrections you think need to be made and any questions you think should be asked. Do not simply send it to your client and ask them to read it. They need your help to interpret what the report says and how it impacts their case. This will be different for each case but the common themes in your letter to your client should be:

- A reminder of who produced the report and what it was to address.
- A reminder that the court ordered the report.
- You have 10 days to ask any questions for clarification and an explanation that clarification is not cross examination.
- Your views on the report.
- What you have to do with the report.

If the report has been commissioned pursuant to a court order, it is the responsibility of the applicant's solicitor to upload the document to the digital portal. The respondent should check that this has been done, since if it has not been done, the respondent should upload it.

If there is a disagreement as to the format of the letter of instruction, the settling of the terms of the letter can be referred back to the court or, preferably, to an arbitrator for a speedy, 'on paper' decision that will not interrupt the court timetable: *CM* v. *CM* [2019] EWFC 16.

# Annex 4A

## Sample questionnaire

IN THE FAMILY COURT CASE NO: XXXX XXXX XXXX XXXX

SITTING AT XXX

In the Matrimonial Causes Act 1973

**Between:**

**MRS JANE DOE**
**Applicant wife**

**And**

**MR JOHN DOE**
**Respondent husband**

---

**DRAFT QUESTIONNAIRE OF THE APPLICANT TO THE RESPONDENT PREPARED FOR APPROVAL AT FIRST APPOINTMENT ON 1 JULY 2024**

---

**Missing documentation**

1. Please produce a copy of your P60 for April 2024.
2. Please produce your tax returns for the last 2 years.

**In respect of Barclays account number XXXXXXX**

3. Please state the nature and purpose of the following payments from this account and provide documentation in support of your reply:

   (a) 01.07.2024: £500.00
   (b) 19.09.2024: £1,000

4. Please state the source, nature and purpose of the following credit payments into this account and provide documentation in support of your reply, to include statements for the last 12 months period if the source of each credit is an account under your control:

   (a) 03.07.2024: £1,000
   (b) 08.08.2024: £1,500

5. Etc...

14.06.2024
ABC SOLICITORS
Solicitors for the applicant

*A note on questionnaires*

Remember that the court controls the evidence and must give permission for you to ask the question in the first instance, so be prepared to have your draft questionnaire scrutinised and importantly, to explain why you are asking that question. The court will not allow a scattergun approach to asking questions and only allows questions that are relevant to the disposal of the application. Remember also that there is a cost for every question asked and answered so they have to be relevant to the issues of the case.

# Annex 4B

## Statement of truth

I believe the contents of my statement are true. I understand that proceedings for contempt of court may be brought against anyone who makes, or causes to be made, a false statement in a document verified by a statement of truth without an honest belief in its truth.

SIGNED: ______________________________

DATED: ____________________

# Annex 4C

## Letter to the client before the First Appointment

Dear [*name of client*]

As you know we are due to attend the Family Court at [*name and address of court*] on [*date and time*]. This is the first hearing of [your] *or* [*name of spouse*]'s application for financial remedy. The court hearing will essentially be used for case management, to make sure that the court has all of the information and documentation that is needed for the FDR – negotiation hearing.

As we have exchanged the required paperwork with [*name of spouse*], we now need to prepare for the hearing.

### The first hearing

Although your hearing is at [*time*] it is a good idea for you to get there early so you can speak to [me] *or* [your advocate/your barrister] and discuss your case. Please make sure that you arrive at the Family Court no later than [*time*]. It may be possible to agree a number of matters in advance of seeing the Judge, which would be a good use of the time you have at court.

On the day, a number of cases will all be listed at the same time before the same Judge. This means that you could be at Court [all morning/all afternoon/all day]. Please ensure that you make appropriate arrangements to be at Court for this length of time.

You can bring someone to Court to support you if you think this will be helpful. Only the parties and their representatives are allowed into the court room but there is a waiting area for anyone who comes with you. [As your spouse is not represented by a lawyer, [he/she] might make an application for a friend to enter the court room to make notes for [him/her]. [He/she] has not yet made this application but might do so on the day. Your advocate will deal with the application if one is made.]

You will not have to give formal evidence at this hearing. Your advocate will speak to the Judge and the other side for you.

### *Representation at the hearing*

[I propose to represent you at the hearing. I estimate my costs of attending will be [£X], and I will therefore need you to place [£X] on account of costs. This should cover my preparation for the hearing, travel and attendance at the hearing. As you know I charge an hourly rate of [£X] and you will be paying for my time to attend.]

OR

[My colleague [*insert name and status of advocate*] will represent you at the hearing. I estimate [his/her] costs of attending to be [£X], and I will therefore need you to place [£X] on account of costs. This should cover preparation for the hearing, travel and attendance at the hearing. [He/she] charges an hourly rate of [£X] and you will be paying for [his/her] time to attend.]

OR

[I propose to instruct a barrister to attend the hearing to represent you. I will send them the necessary paperwork before the hearing with an outline of the matter. I will also try to speak to them about the case in advance. The barrister I have booked is [*insert name and web profile*]. I am confident that [he/she] will be able to represent you very well on the day. [His/her] costs are fixed at [£X plus VAT]. In addition, [*insert name and status*] will also attend the hearing to assist your barrister. I estimate [his/her] costs to be [£X]. I will therefore need you to pay [£X] on account by no later than [*date*].]

We may be able to settle this case before the hearing which would lead to us asking the Court to cancel the hearing and approve the settlement instead. Also, it is always possible that the Court will experience some difficulty which means that the case is removed from the Court hearing list. This happens from time to time and there is nothing we can do to stop the Court from doing this.

If your case does not go ahead as planned on the [*date*] then you may still have to pay the barrister's fees. I have been told that if we cancel your barrister before [*insert date when the deemed fee becomes due*] then no fee will be payable. If we cancel after this date then the full fee will have to be paid.

If you are being represented by [me] *or* [*name of colleague*] you will only be charged for the actual time we spend on the preparation of your case.

## *Bundles*

[As [you are the applicant in this matter] *or* [your spouse does not have a solicitor in this matter] I need to prepare a bundle of documents for the hearing. This is a straightforward matter at this early stage. I will prepare the paperwork and send it to the court and to the other side once it has been agreed.]

OR

[As [*name of spouse*] is the applicant in this matter, [his/her] solicitor needs to prepare a bundle of documents for the hearing. I will contact them to ensure we get these papers before the hearing, as we have an opportunity to agree the content of the bundle before it is sent to the Judge.]

If you have any questions about the hearing please let me know.

# Annex 4D

## Letter to the client enclosing the First Appointment order

Dear [*name of client*]

I enclose a copy of the order made by the Judge at the First Appointment hearing on [*date*]. As you know there are a number of things that both you and [*name of spouse*] must do before the next hearing [*insert date of hearing if known*]. [*Set out the timetable of what needs to be done, by when and by whom.*]

### Answers to questionnaire

The Judge has said that you must answer [*name of client*]'s questionnaire by no later than [*date*]. I attach a copy of the questionnaire that you must answer; some questions were not allowed to be asked by the Judge and these have been deleted. Please let me have your answers and documents by [*date*] so that I can prepare the document and send it to you to check and sign.

### Valuation expert

The Judge has said that if you can both agree a value of the family home by [*date*] then we can use that value at the next hearing. If not, then we will need to ask an expert to prepare a valuation report.

[*Name of spouse*] has suggested that the value is [£X] and you have said that you think it is [£X]. Are you willing to propose a compromise figure to be used at the next hearing? If so, please let me know and I will propose the figure to the other side.

If not, we will need to find three valuation experts who will be able to prepare report for court purposes. We have used the valuers listed below in the past and I am happy to approach them to see how much they would charge to prepare a valuation report in this case. As you know, the costs of the valuation report would be split equally between you both.

1.
2.
3.

### Pension report

The Judge has directed that we obtain a report from a pension expert. We need to propose three pension experts to the other side and the other party can choose one person from these. That person will be appointed as the Court's expert rather than for either of you, and both parties will pay the costs of the report equally.

We need to propose three pension experts by [*date*], and [*name of spouse*] will choose one of the proposed experts. I suggest the three experts listed below, who are all suitably qualified to produce this type of report. I have contacted them to find out if they can prepare a report in the time frame given by the Court. Each expert has confirmed that they are available to prepare the report and they have given me an estimate of their costs based on the information we have.

1. [*Insert name, qualification and costs*].
2. [*Insert name, qualification and costs*].
3. [*Insert name, qualification and costs*].

Please let me know if you are happy for me to propose the above pension experts.

I will need to draft a letter to the pension expert by [*date*]. I will start to draft the letter to send to the other side as [he/she] needs to approve and sign the letter before we send it to the chosen expert.

We shall be allowed to ask further questions when the report is sent out. [*Insert any provision that may have been made on questions to experts.*]

Please let me know if you have any questions regarding these matters.

# Annex 4E

## Letter of instruction to property valuer

Dear Colleagues

Re: *[insert property address]*

This letter is written as a joint instruction to you as an expert in financial remedy proceedings relating to divorce proceedings between [*client's full name*] and [*spouse's full name*]. You are being instructed jointly by [*lead firm preparing letter*] who act on behalf of [*client's full name*] and [*name and address of spouse's solicitors*], [*telephone number and email of spouse's solicitors*] on behalf of [*spouse's full name*], but on the basis that you will provide an expert opinion independent of each of them.

At the First Appointment on [*date of First Appointment*], District Judge [*name*] sitting at the Family Court at [*location*] made the following order [*insert exact wording from order*].

The parties have agreed that you should be instructed on a joint basis as the single joint expert.

Your scope of instructions is as set out in the order dated [*date of First Appointment order*] and in this letter.

### Arrangements for preparing the report

Should you need to discuss the report, either on a preliminary basis or on a more extended basis, please contact both solicitors by joint email.

Please do not discuss any issues direct with either party. Please note that you should not take into account in your report any direct or indirect communication you have with either party, although you should keep records of these communications. Please direct any queries you may have to both parties' solicitors.

[[Mr/Mrs XXX] is in occupation of the property and you should contact them on [*phone number*] to arrange for access to the property.]

### Background information

[*Insert relevant background information, e.g. as to any planning consents or lease agreements in relation to the property etc.*]

## Documents

Please find enclosed the following documents [*amend as appropriate*]:

1. a copy of the order dated [*date of First Appointment order*]
2. relevant extracts from our client's Form E (and documents in support);
3. relevant extracts from other party's Form E (and documents in support);
4. relevant extracts from our client's replies to questionnaire (and documents in support);
5. relevant extracts from other party's replies to questionnaire (and documents in support);
6. [planning consent dated [*insert date*];
7. tenancy agreement granted on the [*insert date*];
8. lease agreement dated [*insert date*];
9. relevant option agreements [*insert details*].]

## Valuation

You are asked to give your opinion as to the open market value of [*identify land or property*] assuming a sale between a willing buyer and a willing seller taking into account [*amend as appropriate*]:

(a) size and nature of the [land/property];
(b) appropriate comparable [land/property];
(c) location and proximity to amenities;
(d) general condition and decorative state;
(e) any particular limitations, tenancies or other arrangements that may affect the [land/property];
(f) any planning permissions, potential planning issues and possible alternative uses together with any potential value from the development or commercial exploitation or recreational development to the extent that it forms an element of the fair market value;
(g) occupations [although if the [land/property] is occupied by any family interest, it should be valued on a vacant possession basis];
(h) impact of neighbouring property issues;
(i) any option agreements;
(j) the scope for water or mineral extraction, if appropriate; and
(k) the 'marriage value' of the land, if appropriate.

The valuation date should be taken as the date of your valuation report and based on the open market value assuming [*amend as appropriate*]:

- a willing buyer and a willing seller;
- a reasonable period for marketing;
- that the state of the market, levels of value and other circumstances remain constant throughout the period of marketing; and
- the valuation is of the land as a whole.

[Please note that a structural survey [is/is not] required.]

## Form of report

Your report must be prepared in accordance with Family Procedure Rules 2010, SI 2010/2955, Part 25 and Practice Directions (PDs) PD 25B, PD 25D and PD 25E. We would draw your attention in particular to paragraph 9.1 of PD 25B which deals with the contents of the report. The report must contain, for example, the following:

1. details of your qualifications and experience;
2. a statement identifying the document(s) containing the material instructions and the substance of any oral instructions and, as far as necessary to explain any opinions or conclusions expressed in the report, summarising the facts and instructions which are material to the conclusions and opinions expressed;
3. details of who carried out any test, examination or interview to which you have referred in your report, to include the qualifications of that person and confirming whether or not the test, examination or interview has been carried out under your supervision;
4. when expressing an opinion, all material facts should be considered and the facts, literature and other material relied upon in forming your opinion should be identified;
5. a description of your own professional risk assessment process and process of differential diagnosis, highlighting factual assumptions, deductions from the factual assumptions and any unusual, contradictory or inconsistent features of the case;
6. a statement indicating whether your opinion is provisional (or qualified, as the case may be) stating the qualification and the reason for it and identifying what further information is required to give an opinion without qualification; and
7. where there is a range of opinion, please:

    (a) summarise the range of opinion;
    (b) identify and explain, within the range of opinions, any 'unknown cause', whether arising from the facts of the case or from limited experience or lack of research, peer review or support in the relevant field of expertise;
    (c) give reasons for any opinion expressed: the use of a balance sheet approach to factors that support or undermine an opinion can be of great assistance to the court;

8. a summary of your conclusions and opinions;
9. you must include a statement in your report that you:

    (a) understand your duty to the court and that you have complied with that duty;
    (b) are aware of the requirements of the Family Procedure Rules 2010, SI 2010/2955, Part 25 and Practice Directions PD 25B, PD 25D and PD 25E; and
    (c) have no conflict of interest of any kind, other than as disclosed in your report, and that you do not consider any interest disclosed as affecting your suitability as an expert witness on any issue on which you have given evidence and that you will advise the parties if, between the date of your report and the final hearing, there is any change in circumstances in relation to the issue of conflict of interest.

10. the report must be verified by the following statement of truth:

> I confirm that I have made clear which facts and matters referred to in this report are within my own knowledge and which are not. Those that are within my own knowledge I confirm to be true. The opinions I have expressed represent my true and complete professional opinions on the matters to which they refer.

If you knowingly sign a statement of truth that is untrue, you may be held in contempt of court and liable to imprisonment.

Your report should be addressed to [*name and address of court*] and not to the parties or their solicitors; however, one copy of your report should be sent simultaneously to each of our respective firms. The report only needs to be provided in electronic form since the court is digitalised and the [applicant's] solicitor will upload your report to the court portal.

Within 10 days of receipt of your report, either party or their solicitors may put questions in writing to you for the purpose only of clarification of your report. Your answers will be treated as part of your report. If you do not reply to these questions, the court may direct that your evidence cannot be relied on.

If required, you may apply to the court for directions to assist you in carrying out your instructions.

We wish to stress that you should regard yourself as an expert of the court and that, as such, your duty is to the court and not to either of the parties. This duty overrides any obligation to the parties or their solicitors. Each party's solicitors should be consulted in relation to any further enquiries which may arise in relation to the preparation of your report.

## Costs of your report

You have confirmed that your fee for carrying out this work will be [*fee*] plus VAT. If it becomes clear that you are likely to exceed this fee, please contact both solicitors as soon as possible with your revised estimate.

Please note that both parties will be responsible for your fees and you should invoice them directly. Your fee is to be met equally by the parties. Please provide each party with an invoice for one-half of your total fee. Each party will also be responsible for one-half of your reasonable costs incurred in answering questions on your report.

## Confirmation

We would be grateful if you would confirm:

1. you have no conflict of interest of any kind;
2. the matter is within your range of expertise;

3. you are available to provide the report within the timescale ordered by the court. If you anticipate difficulties in complying with this timescale, please contact both parties solicitors as soon as possiblc;
4. [your fee will be that already agreed and set out in your letter dated [*date*]] *or* [your likely fee of providing your report including VAT and disbursements so that this may be approved in advance by the parties]; and
5. you do not require any further information or documents in order to carry out these instructions; if any further information or documents are required, please supply a list of the material required.

If this matter is not resolved by negotiation, it is possible that you may be required to give evidence at court. We will discuss the necessity for this with you in due course, ascertaining your availability.

We look forward to hearing from you as soon as possible that you can deal with these instructions.

# Annex 4F

## Letter to single joint expert accountant to obtain CGT calculations

Dear Sirs,

**Re: [*Name of applicant*] and [*Name of respondent*]**

**Family Court sitting at [*location*] – Case No [*number*]**

[You are instructed to prepare a report as a single joint expert in financial proceedings ongoing in the Family Court sitting at [*location*].]

OR

[The parties are in the process of negotiating a settlement and are instructing you to prepare a report to be used in those negotiations. In the event that those negotiations break down it is agreed that your report will be used in financial remedy proceedings, when issued.]

### Contact details

| Contact name | Status | Address | Telephone number | Mobile number | Email address |
|---|---|---|---|---|---|
| [name of applicant] | Applicant | | | | |
| [applicant's solicitor] | Applicant's solicitor | | | | |
| [name of respondent] | Respondent | | | | |
| [respondent's solicitor] | Respondent's solicitor | | | | |

### Background information

A) [You are instructed pursuant to an order of District Judge [*name*] at the Family Court sitting at [*location*] on [*date*]. [A copy of that order is attached to this letter] *or* [a copy of that order was sent to you under separate cover as required by FPR 2010, rule 25.18].]

OR

B) [Although there are ongoing divorce proceedings, neither party has issued financial remedy proceedings. Accordingly, you are being instructed to prepare your report to assist the parties [in [mediation/the collaborative law process/arbitration]] *or* [to negotiate a settlement].]

## Your instructions

You are asked to prepare a report to calculate the Capital Gains Tax that the [applicant] and/or [respondent] would pay upon the disposal of their interests in the following assets:

1. [*Address of property.*] This property is owned by [*name*] and [*name*] in [*shares*]. The property was purchased on [*date of purchase*] for [*price of purchase*].The current value of the property is [*insert value*]. This was the principal residence of the parties until [*date*] when [*insert address*] became the primary residence.
2. [*Address of property.*] This property is owned by [*name*] and [*name*] in [*shares*]. The property was purchased on [*date of purchase*] for [*price of purchase*]. The current value of the property is [*insert value*]. The [applicant/respondent] moved out of this property on [*date*]; however, the [respondent/applicant] remains there and this is [his/her] family home.
3. [*Address of property.*] This property is owned by [*name*] and [*name*] in [*shares*]. The property was purchased on [*date of purchase*] for [*price of purchase*]. The current value of the property is [*insert value*].
4. [*Insert details of any improvement works to the property that would reduce CGT.*]

If you have any questions in respect of these instructions please email the solicitors in the first instance. [You should note that you are entitled to file written requests for directions with the court: FPR 2010, rule 25.17.]

The court now operates digitally. Your report should be addressed to the court but sent only to the solicitors for each party who will upload the document to the digital court portal.

## Your report

You are asked to ensure that your report complies with the requirements set out in FPR 2010, Part 25 (**www.justice.gov.uk/courts/procedure-rules/family/parts/part_25**).

1. Rule 25.14 sets out the contents of your report and directs you to have regard to the requirements set out in Practice Direction 25B, specifically para.9.1.
2. The report must be addressed to the Family Court sitting at [*location*] and not to either of the instructing firms or parties.
3. Please ensure that your report is verified by a statement of truth in the following form:

   I confirm that I have made clear which facts and matters referred to in this report are within my own knowledge and which are not. Those that are within my own knowledge I confirm to be true. The opinions I have expressed represent my true and complete professional opinions on the matters to which they refer.

As you are appointed as a single joint expert, it is important to preserve your impartiality. Please ensure that you do not enter into correspondence or have conversations with one party or their adviser without copying the other party, or making a note which should be appended to your report.

### Timetable

Your report is due to be filed by [*date*]. If you find that you are unable to file the report with the Court by that date, please contact the Court and both solicitors to inform us of a realistic date when the report will be filed.

For your information the next hearing of this matter is on [*date*]. You are not required to attend to give evidence at the hearing.

The parties are permitted to ask questions about your report. These questions should be filed within [10] days of the report being filed. We would ask that you answer those questions by [*insert date or days*].

The cost of answering these questions should be paid for by [the person raising those questions] *or* [both parties equally].

### The paperwork

We enclose the following documentation to assist you to prepare your report:

1. A copy of the order dated [*date*].
2. Valuation report for property [1/2/3].
3. Office copy entries for property [1/2/3].
4. Completion statements for property [1/2/3].
5. [Invoices for improvement works.]

### Your fees

A) [Prior to the preparation of your report or carrying out any preliminary work, please provide us with an estimate of your costs. Once your fees are agreed, please prepare your report.]

OR

B) [You have estimated your fees to be £X, and those fees are accepted by the parties. If there is likely to be an increase in those fees for any reason, please contact us before any additional work is undertaken to ensure that those fees are agreed.]

It has been [ordered by the Court] *or* [agreed by the parties] that they will each be responsible for one half of your costs. We would therefore ask that you [invoice both *name of solicitors* and *name of other solicitors*] *or* [prepare an invoice addressed to each party] for one half of your costs.

| Yours sincerely | Yours sincerely |
|---|---|
| ............................................. | ............................................. |
| [*Name of solicitors*] | [*Name of solicitors*] |
| Solicitors for [applicant] | Solicitors for [respondent] |

*Note*

'Accountant' is not a protected title so make sure that the accountant you instruct is a chartered accountant whose status will be recognised by the court, as opposed to a bookkeeper or person without formal qualifications.

# Annex 4G

## Letter to single joint expert forensic/business accountant

Dear Sirs,

**Re: [*Name of applicant*] and [*Name of respondent*]**

**Family Court sitting at [*location*] – Case No. [*number*]**

[You are instructed to prepare a report as a single joint expert in financial proceedings ongoing in the Family Court sitting at [*location*].]

OR

[The parties are in the process of negotiating a settlement and are instructing you to prepare a report to be used in those negotiations. In the event that those negotiations break down, it is agreed that your report will be used in financial remedy proceedings, when issued.]

### Contact details

| Contact name | Status | Address | Telephone number | Mobile number | Email address |
|---|---|---|---|---|---|
| [name of applicant] | Applicant | | | | |
| [applicant's solicitor] | Applicant's solicitor | | | | |
| [name of respondent] | Respondent | | | | |
| [respondent's solicitor] | Respondent's solicitor | | | | |
| [name] | Company accountant | | | | |
| [name] | Company secretary | | | | |
| [name] | Financial director | | | | |

### Background information

A) [You are instructed pursuant to an order of District Judge [*name*] at the Family Court sitting at [*location*] on [*date*]. [A copy of that order is attached to this letter] *or* [a copy of that order was sent to you under separate cover as required by FPR 2010, rule 25.18].]

OR

B) [Although there are ongoing divorce proceedings, neither party has issued financial remedy proceedings. Accordingly, you are being instructed to prepare your report to assist the parties [in [mediation/the collaborative law process/arbitration]] *or* [to negotiate a settlement].]

## Background of the business

The business is a [limited company/partnership/sole trading business] which was set up by [*name*] on [*date*].

The business specialises in [*insert brief details*].

The applicant [is a [X%] shareholder/director/partner/has no interest in the business] and the respondent [is a [X%] shareholder/director/partner/has no interest in the business].

[*Insert other relevant information about the business.*]

## Your instructions

You are asked to prepare a report providing your opinion on:

1. The value of the company [and the parties' respective interests].
2. Any taxation issues for the applicant and respondent if they were to sell their shares in the business in the tax year [YY/YY]. Please assume that they both have full CGT allowances.
3. Please give your opinion on liquidity:
   (a) How can money be drawn from the business? Please include the tax consequences for each method.
   (b) What is the maximum sum that can be withdrawn from the business in the next 6–12 months?
   (c) Can the company raise finance to enable one party to purchase the other's interest?
   (d) What is the maintainable future income that [*name*] can draw from the business assuming that [*name*] has no further interest in the business?
   (e) Are there any other issues that need to be addressed that are relevant to the business that should be noted in these proceedings?

If you have any questions in respect of these instructions please email the solicitors in the first instance. [You should note that you are entitled to file written requests for directions with the Court: FPR 2010, rule 25.17.]

The court now operates digitally. Your report should be addressed to the court but sent only to the solicitors for each party who will upload the document to the digital court portal.

## Your report

You are asked to ensure that your report complies with the requirements set out in FPR 2010, Part 25 (**www.justice.gov.uk/courts/procedure-rules/family/parts/part_25**).

1. Rule 25.14 sets out the contents of your report and directs you to have regard to the requirements set out in Practice Direction 25B, specifically para.9.1.
2. The report must be addressed to the Family Court sitting at [*location*] and not to either of the instructing firms or parties.
3. Please ensure that your report is verified by a statement of truth in the following form:

> I confirm that I have made clear which facts and matters referred to in this report are within my own knowledge and which are not. Those that are within my own knowledge I confirm to be true. The opinions I have expressed represent my true and complete professional opinions on the matters to which they refer.

As you are appointed as a single joint expert, it is important to preserve your impartiality. Please ensure that you do not enter into correspondence or have conversations with one party or their adviser without copying the other party, or making a note which should be appended to your report.

## Timetable

Your report is due to be filed by [*date*]. If you find that you are unable to file the report with the Court by that date, please contact the Court and both solicitors to inform us of a realistic date when the report will be filed.

For your information the next hearing of this matter is on [*date*]. You are not required to attend to give evidence at the hearing.

The parties are permitted to ask questions about your report. These questions should be filed within [10] days of the report being filed. We would ask that you answer those questions by [*insert date or days*].

The cost of answering these questions should be paid for by [the person raising those questions] *or* [both parties equally].

## The paperwork

We enclose the following documentation to assist you to prepare your report:

1. Form E pages.
2. Business accounts.
3. Evidence to support business valuation.
4. [other].

### Further information or documents

If you need any further information you should contact any of the company personnel listed above.

Please copy the parties' solicitors into any requests for information as you are appointed as the single joint expert in this matter.

### Your fees

A) [Prior to the preparation of your report or carrying out any preliminary work, please provide us with an estimate of your costs. Once your fees are agreed, please prepare your report.]

OR

B) [You have estimated your fees to be £X, and those fees are accepted by the parties. If there is likely to be an increase in those fees for any reason, please contact us before any additional work is undertaken to ensure that those fees are agreed.]

It has been [ordered by the Court] *or* [agreed by the parties] that they will each be responsible for one half of your costs. We would therefore ask that you [invoice both *name of solicitors* and *name of other solicitors*] *or* [prepare an invoice addressed to each party] for one half of your costs.

Yours sincerely

..............................................

[*Name of solicitors*]

Solicitors for [applicant]

Yours sincerely

..............................................

[*Name of solicitors*]

Solicitors for [respondent]

# 5 Financial dispute resolution

## 5.1 Introduction

Realistically, for the vast majority of cases, the financial dispute resolution (FDR) appointment will be the last critical attempt to get the case resolved and settled, before the only option is a contested hearing before the court.

From the outset of your matter, you should have been looking forward and considering how the matter could be settled and what your likely position will be.

### *5.1.1 Between First Appointment and FDR appointment*

There will have been directions made at First Appointment, which should be complied with in good time prior to the FDR appointment, for you to consider with your client what proposals you will make to settle the case. You should have dealt with disclosure, valuations, pension reports, updating financial disclosure, updated particulars for housing need and updated mortgage capacity information. You should have asked any questions that are needed to clarify any expert reports.

You will be collating all of this information and considering what resolution you would make if you were the judge. If you are going to have counsel involved, now is the time to do it, before you make a proposal to settle.

The precedents in this chapter deal with the start of negotiations and matters up to the FDR hearing. It is assumed that the other party is represented rather than a litigant in person. If the other party is not represented, the letters to the other party should be adapted to take this into account. It is always worthwhile negotiating with a litigant in person, and the letters to them need to be clear about the terms of any offer and the potential costs of implementing the proposal.

Initially, negotiations are likely to be conducted on a 'without prejudice' basis. There is nothing to stop practitioners from writing 'open' letters to settle early on and this approach is to be commended, as long as the offers are reasonable. Naturally, once an open offer has been made, it is on the table for the court to see. Consider also alternatives to written correspondence. Is there a place for a round table meeting, remote or otherwise? Is there a place for mediation, with or without solicitors? What are the areas of dispute? Do you have a long wait for an FDR hearing? Could you consider a private FDR? Could you consider an Early Neutral Evaluation session? (If you have got to this stage, a private FDR would be the better option.)

Financial remedy settlement letters should not be marked 'without prejudice save as to costs', or even worse '*Calderbank* v. *Calderbank*', as these will have no effect on costs in financial remedy proceedings, unless negotiating interim applications such as maintenance pending suit. These references are outdated.

The costs rules can be found at FPR 2010, Part 28 and Practice Direction 28A. The ordinary rule in financial remedy proceedings is that each party will pay their own costs: FPR 2010, rule 28.3(5). It is possible for a costs order to be made but this is rare in practice. The provisions that the court must take into account when considering whether to make a costs order are at FPR 2010, rule 28.3(7). Be mindful of the changes introduced in April 2024 placing a greater emphasis on the need to consider and use non-court dispute resolution (NCDR) where appropriate. It is not unreasonable to expect that cost consequences will follow should a party be unreasonable in their refusal to use NCDR.

## 5.2 Without prejudice letter to settle

There are differing styles in forming without prejudice letters. You will generally be writing an open letter at the same time, so bear that in mind. You may not need to repeat what is in an open letter.

Typically, the proposal letter will be some 'highlights' of points or issues that explain why the offer is being made. Then will come the offer.

The key point in formulating this offer is to be clear, to have it not only approved but also understood by your client, and to include a statement regarding any particular issues.

Your offer should cover income, capital, property and pensions, as well as when the right to make financial claims should terminate. You could follow the standard order template in simpler form to ensure that you have covered all areas.

Bear in mind that even when you are writing to a fellow practitioner, in reality, you are writing to the other party since it is most likely that the solicitor will simply forward on a copy of your letter, with their accompanying advice. Be aware of the Language Matters report and recommendations from the Family Solutions Group, supported by the President of the Family Division. Use the parties' names and simple language where possible.

It is sensible to send a schedule of assets and income so that there is no confusion as to the precise assets and value of those assets at the time when the offer is made. If no schedule is sent then the letter itself will need to outline the assets, and it is recommended that you use the ES2 to do this, updated from the version used at the First Appointment.

It is always helpful to include in your letter a 'net effect' table, showing how the assets would fall per your proposal and the percentage split between the parties for non-pension assets and assets overall, including pension assets.

In the body of the letter, neutral terminology is used to put forward a proposal which should always include relevant time limits, costs and undertakings if required. In this precedent, it is proposed that a jointly owned home is transferred from joint names into the wife's sole name although she is unable to release the husband from his mortgage covenants. It is not unusual in case negotiations for one party to want to transfer the property without being able to release the other from the mortgage. At the minimum, the mortgage company will probably need to give consent to transfer the property even if the mortgage is not transferred. Alternatively, the property could remain in the parties' joint names, in which case the beneficial ownership would be declared in the order (this is known as a 'Mesher' order).

In the without prejudice letter in **Annex 5A**, the wife has agreed to pay the monthly mortgage payments and other outgoings, and has agreed to indemnify the husband against any breach of the mortgage covenants. She has also agreed to give an undertaking to use her best endeavours to release him from the mortgage as soon as possible. In the letter in **Annex 5B** the implications of the offer are explained to the husband as the undertaking is difficult to enforce and the indemnity would only be used after the mortgage company has recouped arrears from him. He would then enforce the indemnity against the wife but this would only be fruitful if she had assets against which he could enforce. It is possible that this could be effected against her share of the equity in the family home.

It is important to note that the offer should be clear about the way that net equity is calculated. The method will either be:

1. the equity share now expressed as a percentage of the market value of the property now, so that the receiver has the benefit of any latent rise in the value of the property – but not the increase in equity due to paying down the mortgage; or
2. the net equity after deduction from the value of the property of the mortgage outstanding, the estate agent's commission on sale and the solicitor's fees for conveyancing, plus any CGT to be paid.

*Example*

Value of property: £300,000

Mortgage redemption (today's figure): £123,456

Costs of sale (2.5%): £7,500

Total equity = £169,044

35% = £59,165.40

If switching to use the gross equity figure for 35%, take the cash sum due to the recipient, which in this example is £59,165, and represent it as against the value of the property, which is £300,000. This means that the recipient is entitled to 19.72% of the gross value of the property.

If the husband gets his share when the property is worth £400,000 in five years' time, under the net calculation he would receive:

Property value: £400,000

Mortgage: £123,456

Costs of sale (2.5%): £10,000

Net equity = £266,544

**35% = £93,290.40**

Using the gross equity calculation in five years' time against a property worth £400,000:

Property value: £400,000

**19.72% of property value = £78,880**

That is a loss to the recipient of **£14,410.40**, just by converting the net sum into a gross figure.

Paragraph 6 sets out the events upon which the husband can expect to receive his money. These are often referred to as 'trigger events', and all of these events are subject to negotiation. Many courts do not allow a trigger event that is referable to one party's cohabitation. Cohabitation can be a difficult matter to prove and it requires the parties to have a high degree of interaction with each other after the divorce, which can be intrusive and unwanted. Further, the financial obligations to a former spouse and children are not transferred to a cohabitee. The need for housing is still there, whether there is a cohabitee or not.

As the property is being secured as a home for the benefit of the children, it is unusual for the husband's charge to be paid to him while the children are still minors. Paragraph 7 makes it very clear that even if one of the trigger events occurs, the husband will not receive his money if the children are still minors and in full-time education or training.

It appears that the parties have agreed that the husband will pay school fees and reasonable extras. It is sensible to set out what those extras will be or how they will be agreed in the future. The husband is to pay the fees for the children's current schools or any schools that they may attend in future by mutual agreement.

The wife would like spousal maintenance to be paid at a fixed rate of £1,000 per calendar month subject to an annual variation referable to Consumer Price Index (CPI) increases. In the alternative, she could ask for annual variation referable to Retail Price Index (RPI) increases or a fixed percentage increase, which is much more unusual to see in financial remedy orders.

It is important to state whether the wife will be entitled to apply for an extension of the maintenance term. If it is not intended that she will be able to extend the term, an MCA 1973, s.28(1A) bar should be imposed and specifically referred to in the offer letter. Paragraph 11 makes it clear that she will be allowed to apply for an extension.

The responsibility to pay the costs of any pension sharing implementation should be set out in the offer. If this is overlooked then the costs will be the responsibility of the transferor in their entirety.

The matter of the house contents and personal belongings should always be addressed. If the parties have not already divided these, they will need to draw up lists of the items that they want to keep and these would form part of the negotiations.

Paragraphs 15 and 16 deal with the clean break provisions. The wife cannot have a clean break on income until her maintenance term has expired. She is therefore entitled to make an application during that time under the Inheritance (Provision for Family and Dependants) Act 1975.

The client proposes that each party will pay their own costs, and this is in line with the general costs provision for financial remedy cases. However, it appears that a costs order was made in respect of the divorce proceedings and it was agreed that the husband would pay costs at the rate of £1,500. Although this is part of the divorce proceedings, it is possible to use this as a negotiating matter in the financial remedy proceedings.

It is usual for there to be liberty to apply in respect of timing and implementation.

## 5.3 Letter to the client advising on the without prejudice offer

This letter (**Annex 5B**) is sent with reference to the offer made in the letter at **Annex 5A**. When sending an offer to settle to the client, it is quite important to present it in either neutral or positive terms. If it is a first offer which is not one which the client would be likely to accept, it should be presented to the client with suggestions of possible areas where it might be possible to negotiate a better settlement. It may even be a good idea to meet with the client before giving them a copy of the letter – in that way the terms of the offer can be discussed in person, hopefully avoiding the client reacting badly to the contents of the letter.

If you can explain to the client why the offer is made in potentially unfavourable terms, this is an important message for them to hear. In this case, the offer is made on the basis that the wife and children will remain in the family home. If you know that the client wants the family home to be sold this should be addressed when presenting the offer letter to the client.

If clients have unreasonable expectations of the settlement, they should be informed of the most likely outcomes. This is a delicate line to tread: on the one hand, you do not want to allow the client hold unreasonable expectations but, on the other hand, the client is entitled to give instructions to settle; that may not immediately accord with the way the court would deal with things. You hope that those initial, unreasonable views will change. This is most likely to happen when the clients have been to the FDR hearing and heard the judge's views on the likely settlement prospects.

The FDR hearing is designed so that the judge conducting the hearing can assess both parties' settlement proposals and help the parties to narrow the areas of dispute. There is a good prospect that the parties will be able to reach a final agreement at the FDR hearing or very soon after the hearing with the help of the judge.

## 5.4 Letter to the client before the financial dispute resolution hearing

The letter to the client before the financial dispute resolution hearing (**Annex 5C**) mirrors the earlier precedent at **Annex 4C** informing the client about the impending hearing, the costs of attendance and the options for representation. In this letter the client is informed that the client will be expected to negotiate a settlement of the financial matters at the FDR hearing.

It is usual to warn the client about the increased costs between the FDR hearing and the final hearing. These costs usually double, at the very least. It is important that the client accounts for the potential costs when considering whether to accept a proposed offer or when making a counter offer at the hearing.

You should bear in mind the importance of instructing counsel at an early stage and possibly having a conference with counsel before the FDR hearing.

The Family Justice Council has produced some very good best practice guidance regarding FDR hearings which should be taken into account. This guidance can be found at **www.judiciary.gov.uk/wp-content/uploads/2014/10/fjc_financial_dispute_resolution.pdf.**

## 5.5 Conclusion

FDR hearings are fraught with tension for clients, who will have spent several months embroiled in court proceedings and spent thousands of pounds on legal representation. Clients usually want to reach a settlement at this hearing but need to be reassured that they are making the right decisions. If the fee earner with conduct of the case is not able to represent the client, it is a good idea for them to be in attendance at the hearing with counsel or available by telephone if the client wants to discuss a proposed settlement.

Clients always feel under pressure to settle and there is always the possibility that the client complains after a successful FDR hearing. Clients should never be forced to enter into an agreement if they are not certain it is what they want.

# Annex 5A

## Without prejudice letter to settle

Without Prejudice

Dear Sirs

We write to you in the hope that the parties may be able to reach a settlement of these matters without the necessity to attend the next hearing on [*date*].

### Background

Our client is [*insert age*] years old and works on a full-time basis as a [*insert occupation*]. She is claiming tax credits and child benefit, and she is therefore maximising her earning capacity. Your client is [*insert age*] years old and also works on a full-time basis as a [*insert occupation*]. He too is maximising his earning capacity. The parties have been in a settled relationship of 15 years, including 5 years of premarital cohabitation.

The attached schedule of assets and income shows the parties' respective positions. It is clear that there is a substantive disparity between their net income positions.

The children are [*insert name of child and age*] and [*insert name of child and age*]. Both live with their mother at the family home and have substantive contact with their father.

Both parties have agreed that they would like the children to continue to attend their current schools, and this will therefore mean that money will need to be found to pay their school fees.

### Our offer

Our client has instructed us to propose the following, on the basis that the children remain in the family home which is nearby to their schools.

1. The jointly owned family home be transferred to our client, subject to the current mortgage. The transfer shall take place within 28 days of the sealed consent order being received by the parties.
2. Our client is not in a position to release your client from his covenants under the mortgage. However, she is willing to take over the payments for the mortgage immediately. In addition, she is willing to offer an indemnity to your client in respect of the mortgage obligations.
3. She will also give him an undertaking to use her best endeavours to release him from the mortgage as soon as possible.
4. Your client will register a charge against the property upon completion of the transfer; this will be to secure his share of the net equity at 35%.

5. The net equity of the property will be calculated as the value of the property minus the mortgage at the date of the agreement. This currently stands at [*insert redemption figure*], less the costs of sale fixed at 2.5%.
6. Your client can expect to be paid the monies secured by way of charge, upon the occurrence of the first event listed below:

   (a) the youngest child of the family finishing his full-time secondary education or attaining the age of 18 years (whichever is the later);
   (b) the death of the applicant;
   (c) the applicant remarrying or cohabiting with another person as husband-and-wife for a continuous period of more than 12 months;
   (d) the applicant's failure to occupy the property for a period of 3 months in any 12-month period;
   (e) the applicant's failure to occupy the property as her primary residence;
   (f) further order.

7. The events that trigger the payment of your client's money shall not be exercisable without permission of the court while any child of the family in occupation of the property is still a minor or of full age but receiving full-time education or training.
8. Your client will pay all school fees and reasonable extras as appearing on the school bill. These shall be paid as and when demanded by the school. This obligation shall be in respect of both children for the schools they currently attend or any school that the parties agree the children should attend in the future.
9. Your client will pay child maintenance at the figure assessed by the Child Maintenance Service.
10. Your client will pay spousal maintenance for our client at the rate of £1,000 per calendar month. Such maintenance will be paid until the occurrence of the first of the following events:

    (a) the youngest child of the family finishing full-time secondary education or attaining the age of 18, whichever is the later;
    (b) the death of the applicant or respondent;
    (c) the applicant cohabiting with another person as husband-and-wife for a continuous period of more than 12 months;
    (d) further order.

11. The applicant may apply for an order to extend this term.
12. The spousal maintenance payments shall be varied annually in line with any increase of the Consumer Price Index (CPI).
13. There shall be a 42% pension sharing order in favour of the applicant. The parties will pay the costs of the trustees for pension sharing implementation equally. This is in line with pension expert's report.
14. The parties have divided the contents of the family home between them. If there are any personal items that your client wishes to take he should provide a list of these for our client's consideration.
15. There shall be a clean break in respect of your client's claims against ours in life and death.

16. There shall be a clean break in respect of our client's claims, save for her income claims which will remain open until expiration of the term. When our client's maintenance comes to an end she will no longer be able to make an application under the Inheritance (Provision for Family and Dependants) Act 1975, s.2.
17. Each party shall pay their own costs in respect of the financial remedy proceedings. There is a costs order that your client is to pay the costs of divorce. We agreed to cap these costs at £1,500. The costs should be paid within 14 days of the final divorce order being pronounced.
18. There shall be liberty to apply.

## Net effect

The above offer is designed to minimise any disruption to the children, which the parties both agree is their goal. Our client will remain in the family home and we accept that until she is able to release your client from his covenants under the joint mortgage, he is unlikely to be able to purchase another property. He is currently living in rented accommodation and although he would like to purchase a property this is not likely to be possible until he receives his share of the net equity in the family home.

Your client will receive net equity of 35%. The small departure away from equality is to reflect the money that he withdrew from the parties' joint savings account when he left the family home. This money was used to pay the deposit at the property he currently rents and the first month's rent. He will receive the deposit money back when he vacates the property. Save for that one small adjustment, the above offer reflects an equal division of the property and pensions.

You will note from the attached schedule of assets that your client will be left with 40% of his net income, after he has paid the school fees and child and spousal maintenance as per the terms of the order. His net income will allow him to pay his rent and reasonable costs of living as per his outgoings schedule.

We believe that the above offer is fair to both the parties as they will both continue to maintain a standard of living which is similar to that enjoyed by them during the marriage. Our client understands that your client wants to purchase a property rather than rent a property; sadly, the current circumstances do not allow for this.

We should be grateful if you could take your client's instructions and revert to us within 21 days with his response.

# Annex 5B

## Letter to the client advising on the without prejudice offer

Dear [*name of client*]

I am pleased to inform you that we have received an offer to settle from [*name of spouse*]. This is only a first offer but I recommend that we start to think about putting together a counter offer if you decide that you do not want to accept this offer.

### The offer

The attached offer proposes that [*name of spouse*] and the children remain in the family home. I know that you would ideally like the home sold so that you are released from the mortgage but [*name of spouse*] would like to remain living there with the children. She has offered to pay the monthly mortgage instalments and all the outgoings but as you know, she is unable to release you from the mortgage as she doesn't earn enough.

She has offered you an indemnity. This means that if she fails to pay the mortgage she would protect you from any losses you incur if the mortgage company pursue you for the arrears. This will not prevent the mortgage company from making you pay arrears, but it does mean that you could get those back from her, if she has the money to pay you. At this stage we do not know whether the mortgage company will consent to transfer the property from your joint names into her sole name. She will need to make some enquiries about this issue before you can seriously consider her offer.

### Housing needs

I appreciate that this is not the offer you had hoped for; however, this is the only way that she could stay in the family home with the children, which is what she wants. The family home is a three bed semi-detached property so she is not living in a property that is too big for her.

I know that you believe that she could move to a different area and buy a smaller three bed terraced house which would allow her to release you from this mortgage. A judge may not agree that your proposal is sensible or fair. We can hear from the Judge at the financial dispute resolution (FDR) hearing what he/she thinks about it. In the meantime, we can discuss putting this forward as a counter proposal.

### Equity

She is offering you 35% of the net equity in the property, which would be calculated by using the value of the property at the time you were to get your money. The current redemption figure for the mortgage would be deducted, and this means that you would not benefit from any mortgage payments that reduce the sum outstanding to the mortgage company. [*Name of spouse*] should not be able to increase the capital sum outstanding to the mortgage company. In my view, fixing the redemption figure to the current value is fair.

The costs of sale fixed at 2.5% would also be deducted; this is usual although we may be able to negotiate the figure down to 2%. I have prepared an example of the calculation below, based on the value of the property at £300,000.

*Worked example*

Value of property: £300,000

Mortgage redemption (today's figure): £123,456

Costs of sale (2.5%): £7,500

Total equity = £169,044

35% = £59,165.40

Although she indicates that she is offering you an equal share in the property, she has adjusted the division of equity to take into account the money that you withdrew from the joint savings account, by agreement, when you left the house. I understand that you used this money for the first month's rent, six weeks' deposit and some furniture for the property that you are renting, which you will keep. You have previously informed me that you are likely to lose some of the deposit as the children have damaged a doorway with their toys and crayons. Obviously this is a matter that we need to discuss further.

### Pension

She has offered to settle with a pension share in line with the expert's report. I think this is reasonable under the circumstances. She is offering to share the costs of implementation equally.

### Maintenance

She has indicated that she wants you to pay her spousal maintenance of £1,000 per calendar month. This is in additional to child maintenance at the child maintenance service (CMS) rate. I know that you were hoping that you would not need to pay [*name of spouse*] spousal maintenance if she agreed to sell the family home and downsize to a smaller property. If you look at the schedule of assets and income, you can see that you can afford to pay the sum of £1,000 pcm if you reduce your expenditure. She has not offered to reduce her expenditure, which is not extravagant but could be trimmed in places.

## School fees

She says that you have both agreed that the children should continue at their private fee-paying schools and that you will pay the school fees and reasonable extras. Please let me know whether you have agreed this.

## Costs

She has proposed that you will each pay your own legal costs in respect of the financial negotiations but would like you to pay the agreed sum of £1,500 in respect of the divorce costs. An order was made that you pay these costs but we may be able to negotiate this when we prepare a counter offer.

I would ask you to consider the terms of the overall offer and let me know if you would like to accept this offer or whether you would like me to put together a counter offer. It is a good idea to put together an offer as soon as possible as we may be able to settle matters before the next hearing.

I look forward to hearing from you.

# Annex 5C

## Letter to the client before the financial dispute resolution hearing

Dear [*name of client*]

As you know, we are due to attend the Family Court at [*insert name and address of court*] on [*insert date and time*]. This is the financial dispute resolution (FDR) hearing of [your] *or* [*name of spouse*]'s application for financial remedy.

We have now exchanged offers to settle with [*name of spouse*], so we should have some useful negotiations at this hearing.

### The FDR hearing

Although your hearing is at [*time*] it is a good idea for you to get there early so you can speak to [me] *or* [your advocate/your barrister] and discuss your case. Please make sure that you arrive at the Family Court no later than [*time*]. We have been asked to attend the hearing at least one hour in advance of the hearing time so that we can negotiate with [*name of spouse*]'s advocate.

The court will expect you to be ready to negotiate a settlement of these matters on the day, [your representative] will advise you on any offers that [*name of spouse*] makes and whether to accept or make any counter offers. You must consider all offers that are made and seriously consider whether you want to settle or continue with the litigation. The next hearing will be the final hearing. Your costs will at least double between this hearing and the final hearing and you should bear this in mind when you are negotiating at the FDR hearing.

On the day, a number of cases will all be listed at the same time before the same Judge. This means that you could be at court [all morning/all afternoon/all day]. Please ensure that you make appropriate arrangements to be at Court for this length of time.

You can bring someone to Court to support you if you think this will be helpful. Only the parties and their representatives are allowed into the court room but there is a waiting area for anyone who comes with you. [As your spouse is not represented by a lawyer, [he/she] might make an application for a friend to enter the court room to make notes for them. [He/she] has not yet made this application but might do so on the day. Your advocate will deal with the application if one is made.]

You will not have to give formal evidence at this hearing. Your advocate will speak to the Judge and the other side for you.

## Representation at the hearing

[I propose to represent you at the hearing. I estimate my costs of attending will be [£X], and I will therefore need you to place [£X] on account of costs. This should cover my preparation for the hearing, travel and attendance at the hearing. As you know I charge an hourly rate of [£X] and you will be paying for my time to attend.]

OR

[My colleague [*insert name and status*] will represent you at the hearing. I estimate [his/her] costs of attending to be [£X], and I will therefore need you to place [£X] on account of costs. This should cover preparation for the hearing, travel and attendance at the hearing. [He/she] charges an hourly rate of [£X] and you will be paying for [his/her] time to attend.]

OR

[I propose to instruct a barrister to attend the hearing to represent you. I will send them the necessary paperwork before the hearing with an outline of the matter. I will also try to speak to them about the case in advance. The barrister I have booked is [*insert name and web profile*] [who represented you at the first hearing]. I am confident that [he/she] will be able to represent you very well on the day. [His/her] costs are fixed at [£X plus VAT]. In addition, [*insert name and status*] will also attend the hearing to assist your barrister, and I estimate [his/her] costs to be [£X]. I will therefore need you to pay [£X] on account by no later than [*date*].]

It is possible that we will be able to settle this case before the hearing which would lead to us asking the Court to cancel the hearing and approve the settlement instead. Also, it is always possible that the Court will experience some difficulty which means that the case will be removed from the Court hearing list. This happens from time to time and there is nothing we can do to stop the Court from doing this.

[If your case does not go ahead as planned on [*date*] then you may still have to pay the barrister's fees. I have been told that if we cancel your barrister before [*insert date when the deemed fee becomes due*] then no fee will be payable. If we cancel after this date then the full fee will have to be paid.]

[If you are being represented by [me] *or* [*name of colleague*] you will only be charged for the actual time we spend on the preparation of your case.]

## Bundles

[As [you are the applicant in this matter] *or* [your spouse is the applicant but does not have a solicitor in this matter], I need to prepare a bundle of documents for the hearing. This is a straightforward matter at this early stage. I will prepare the paperwork and send it to the court and to the other side once it has been agreed.]

OR

[As [*name of spouse*] is the applicant in this matter, [his/her] solicitor needs to prepare a bundle of documents for the hearing. I will contact them to ensure we get these papers before the hearing, as we have an opportunity to agree the content of the bundle before it is sent to the Judge.]

If you have any questions about the hearing please let me know.

Yours sincerely

# Annex 5D

## Letter to the client sending the FDR order

Dear [*name of client*]

I enclose a copy of the order made by the Judge at the financial dispute resolution (FDR) hearing on [*date*]. Unfortunately you were unable to reach an agreement with [*name of spouse*] on the day. We can continue to negotiate in the hope that we do not need to go to the final hearing.

In the meantime, we must ensure that we deal with those matters that the Judge ordered at the FDR hearing, just in case we do not settle these matters.

### Statements

Both of you have been ordered to file statements before the next hearing to summarise your positions. I will start to prepare the statement which needs to address the legal points that the Judge will take into account when making a decision about the division of finances. Please note that this is not an opportunity to say whatever you like about [*name of spouse*], since the statement needs to deal with a number of specific matters.

Your statements must be exchanged on [*date*], I propose to send you a first draft of the statement by no later than [*date*] and you should be ready to send me an amended version of the statement by [*date*]. I would therefore hope to be able to file the statement on time and exchange it with [*name of spouse*].

### Updated disclosure

The Judge wants you both to update your financial disclosure by [*date*]. This means that you need to provide updated bank statements, credit card statements, payslips, P60, business accounts and any other financial information to ensure that we have a complete picture of your financial circumstances. Much of this information will be used to produce an up-to-date schedule of assets before the final hearing.

The Judge will only see those documents that are very important at the final hearing. The Judge does not need to see every document produced in the disclosure process.

### Updated housing particulars and mortgage capacity

It is important that we have a good idea of the cost of housing for both you and [*name of spouse*]. For this reason, the Judge has indicated that you should produce updated housing information by [*date*]. Please make sure I have these details by no later than [*date*].

As I have informed you previously, it is a good idea to produce full colour estate agents' particulars rather than print black and white property details from a website. The Judge will be given copies of these housing particulars.

I would also encourage you to visit the properties that you are proposing for yourself and for [*name of spouse*]. You are likely to be asked questions at the final hearing about these properties and so it is vital that you have done more than just obtain details from a website.

Although you have already produced a document which shows your mortgage capacity, if your overall income position has changed for the better or worse then you should produce a current mortgage capacity document.

## Updated valuation

The Judge has given us permission to approach the single joint expert property valuer to provide us with an updated property valuation. [*Name of spouse*]'s solicitor and I will arrange for this updated report to be made available by no later than [*date*].

We do not need an updated pension expert's report. The Judge did not give us permission to update the report, which has only just been produced in any event.

We do not yet know the date of the final hearing, and as soon as I know the date I will contact you with it.

# 6 Final hearing

## 6.1 Introduction

The precedents in the Annexes to this chapter deal with preparation up to the final hearing. Most of the work will already have been done but the applicant will need to prepare the trial bundle for the final hearing, and if the applicant is a litigant in person, the first represented respondent will prepare the trial bundle index. It is good practice to provide a copy of the trial bundle to the litigant in person, who should be consulted about the content of the trial bundle. The trial bundle should accord with FPR 2010, Practice Direction 27A. Be mindful also of the President's Direction regarding preparation of electronic bundles with the requirement that the bundles are consecutively paginated, book marked and searchable. The ES1, ES2, witness template and essential reading list should all be agreed where possible.

Unless the court has directed otherwise, the bundle should be no more than 350 pages. For this reason it is sensible to file the Forms E without the attachments unless they are going to be referred to in the hearing. If particular documents will be needed for cross examination (e.g. bank account statements) they need to be included in the bundle.

Both parties should be trying to reach a settlement of matters. If an agreement is reached then a consent order should be drafted and submitted to the court, which is dealt with in **Chapter 7**.

## 6.2 After the FDR hearing

The court will usually want the parties to file statements, sometimes referred to as 'section 25 statements'. The statement will stand as the evidence in chief for each client, although further brief oral evidence is usually permitted. The evidence contained within the statement should refer to MCA 1973, s.25.

The court may order updated property valuations and direct both parties to file updated disclosure. This is either done separately to filing the statement or can sometimes be dealt with within the statement.

The court will require the parties to file updated housing particulars to show appropriate housing for themselves and for the other party. It is imperative that the client produces good quality property particulars, preferably in colour so that the judge has a good idea of the properties that are proposed. Clients should also visit the proposed properties, particularly if they are proposing that property as their children's main housing. They are likely to be cross-examined about the housing particulars, especially if the issue of alternative housing is central to the financial remedy case.

## 6.3 Statement

**Annex 6A** sets out the bare bones of a section 25 statement, structured around the s.25(2) factors (a)–(h) in MCA 1973. Those factors form subheadings with the relevant information included underneath. Each paragraph should be numbered sequentially, each page should be numbered and only information that has not previously been referred to should be included. You should note that this is not a position statement, it is a witness statement which should accord with the requirements at FPR 2010, Practice Direction 22A.

Practice Direction 22A sets out a lot of detail about the preparation of a witness statement. It specifies that where dates and figures are expressed, numbers should be used. Where documents are mentioned these should be noted in the margin or in bold text.

Where exhibits are attached to the statement the first page of each exhibit should be marked in the same way as the first page of the witness statement, noting the details on the top right hand corner of the statement. Occasionally the court will limit the number of pages that the parties may submit in the statements and those limits should be strictly observed.

## 6.4 Open position

The letter at **Annex 6B** follows the outline of the without prejudice letter at **Annex 5A**. The notable difference is that this letter is not marked 'without prejudice'.

In the first paragraph of the letter, it is noted that this is the open proposal to be used at the final hearing. The applicant must file this 14 days in advance of the hearing: FPR 2010, rule 9.28. This letter is much more formal than the without prejudice offer as this will be presented to the court at the final hearing. It would be more usual for the parties to be referred to as 'your client'/'my client' or 'Mr and Mrs X' rather than using their first names in this letter.

You should consider how to adapt this letter if it is being sent to a litigant in person.

The open position should be a realistic offer to settle matters, as the court will take this as a starting point.

The main difference between this letter and the without prejudice letter is that the terms are different, and the terms in this offer are likely to be less advantageous. This means that if there is a without prejudice offer on the table at the same time, it is likely to offer more favourable terms than the open position.

The asset schedule is said to show the net effect position of the offer, which is of great practical assistance to the judge.

The offer now proposes a net equity share of 45% at paragraph 4 but the trigger events at paragraph 6 are now different. The wife is only offering to release the husband's interest when the youngest child finishes full-time tertiary education, to include a gap year. This means that the husband will get his money much later than under the terms of the without prejudice offer, even though he is being offered a larger share.

The wife no longer intends to release his interest if she starts to cohabit, even though this was previously offered on a without prejudice basis.

The wife now proposes that the husband pays both school and university fees at paragraph 8; previously she was content with only school fees being paid.

The wife is now seeking a higher rate of spousal maintenance per calendar month; this is increased by £200 per calendar month and ends when the youngest child finishes full-time tertiary (not secondary) education to include a gap year, or remarriage or the death of either party. Previously, she was willing to accept the termination of her maintenance in the event that she cohabited for a significant period of time.

The net effect reasoning is much the same. It does not refer to the increased time to pay spousal maintenance or receive the net equity in the home. These matters are always subject to negotiation and the court has a wide discretion whether to include these.

Respondents are required to submit their open position seven days after receiving the applicant's open position.

## 6.5 Costs estimate

Form H1 Statement of Costs (financial remedy) is the costs schedule that must be filed prior to the final hearing. This should be filed not less than 14 days before the final hearing: FPR 2010, rule 9.27(2). It is available at **www.gov.uk/government/publications/give-a-statement-of-costs-for-a-financial-remedy-divorce-form-h1**.

Practitioners sometimes overlook this as the Form H only needs to be filed at a hearing and not in advance of it. Form H1 needs to be served on the other party as well as being filed with the court. The format of the Form H1 is similar to that of the Form H, and the first page contains a 'summary of costs' statement.

Section A: this information can be copied over from the Form Hs filed previously as long as those estimates were accurate. It is worth looking over the time recording and bills to ensure that the estimates given previously can be used at this stage.

Section B: all post-issue costs up to and including the FDR appointment should be included. This is a composite of information provided in the first and second Form H filed at the First Appointment and FDR hearing.

Section C: this is new information about the costs incurred after the FDR hearing and up to the date that the form is signed (14 days before the final hearing).

Section D: this is an estimate of costs incurred after the date the form is signed and up to the end of the final hearing.

Section E: this is an estimate of costs of implementation. This estimate should be thought through properly if there are property transfers and pension implementation costs. The costs of implementation can sometimes be quite high and are not always accurately estimated.

If you intend to seek a costs order to be made against the other party, a Form N260 should be filed, available online at **www.gov.uk/government/publications/form-n260-statement-of-costs-summary-assessment**.

## 6.6 Conclusion

The case should be administratively ready for a final hearing. Counsel will need to be instructed in advance of the hearing and having a conference with counsel is very important. Negotiations will continue to the door of the court in the hope that the parties will be able to reach an agreement rather than having an order imposed upon them.

# Annex 6A

## Outline section 25 statement

This statement is filed
on behalf of the applicant
Maker:
Statement no:
Exhibits:
Date made:

IN THE FAMILY COURT CASE NO: XXXX

SITTING AT [*location*]

BETWEEN:

[Name of applicant]

**Applicant**

– and –

[Name of respondent]

**Respondent**

---

**[First] statement of [name]**

---

I [*insert name and address*] make this statement pursuant to an order of [*name of judge*] made on [*date*].

1. The income, earning capacity, property and other financial resources which each of the parties to the marriage has or is likely to have in the foreseeable future, including in the case of earning capacity any increase in that capacity which it would in the opinion of the court be reasonable to expect a party to the marriage to take steps to acquire.
   (a) [*refer to current income and benefits/tax credits and ability to increase income*]
2. The financial needs, obligations and responsibilities which each of the parties to the marriage has or is likely to have in the foreseeable future.
   (a) [*refer to housing particulars and the condition of the proposed housing by other side*]
   (b) [*refer to mortgage capacity and ability to repay the mortgage if relevant*]
3. The standard of living enjoyed by the family before the breakdown of the marriage.
   (a) [*insert brief details to expand on information given in the Form E*]

4. The age of each party to the marriage and the duration of the marriage.
   (a) [*detail any period of cohabitation before the marriage*]
   (b) [*if relevant, set out the date of separation and if there is any dispute expand on the information previously given*]
5. Any physical or mental disability of either of the parties to the marriage.
   (a) [*update on any conditions mentioned in the Form E or any new conditions, attach evidence*]
6. The contributions which each of the parties has made or is likely in the foreseeable future to make to the welfare of the family, including any contribution by looking after the home or caring for the family.
   (a) [*this is probably already covered in the Form E and other statements; if this refers to future contributions then include it here*]
7. The conduct of each of the parties, if that conduct is such that it would in the opinion of the court be inequitable to disregard it.
   (a) [*litigation misconduct can be mentioned here*]
   (b) [*if the other party has spent wantonly during the proceedings this can be mentioned here – subject to taking advice*]
8. In the case of proceedings for divorce or nullity of marriage, the value to each of the parties to the marriage of any benefit ... which, by reason of the dissolution or annulment of the marriage, that party will lose the chance of acquiring.
   (a) [*mention any other matters that might be relevant*]
9. Other circumstances.
   (a) [*the court is obliged to take into account any other matters that might be relevant, and these should be included here*]

## Statement of truth

I believe the contents of my statement are true. I understand that proceedings for contempt of court may be brought against anyone who makes, or causes to be made, a false statement in a document verified by a statement of truth without an honest belief in its truth.

SIGNED: ____________________________

DATED: __________________

# Annex 6B

## Open position

Dear Sirs

We write to you with our client's open proposal prior to the final hearing on [*date*]. We look forward to receiving your client's open position in 7 days or your confirmation that your client will not be making an open proposal.

### Background

Our client is [*age*] years old and works on a full-time basis as a [*occupation*]. She is claiming tax credits and child benefit, and she is therefore maximising her earning capacity. Your client is [*age*] years old and also works on a full-time basis as a [*occupation*]. He too is maximising his earning capacity. The parties have been in a settled relationship of 15 years, including 5 years of premarital cohabitation.

The attached schedule of assets and income shows the parties' respective positions. It is clear that there is a substantive disparity between their net income positions. That schedule also shows the net effect of our open proposal.

The children are [*insert name of child and age*] and [*insert name of child and age*]. Both live with their mother at the family home and have substantive contact with their father.

Both parties have agreed that they would like the children to continue to attend their current schools. This will therefore mean that money will need to be found to pay their school fees.

### Our offer

Our client has instructed us to propose the following, on the basis that the children remain in the family home which is near to their schools.

1. The jointly owned family home shall be transferred to our client, subject to the current mortgage. The transfer shall take place within 28 days of the sealed consent order being received by the parties.
2. Our client is not in a position to release your client from his covenants under the mortgage. However, she is willing to take over the payments for the mortgage immediately. In addition, she is willing to offer an indemnity to your client in respect of the mortgage obligations.
3. She shall also give him an undertaking to use her best endeavours to release him from the mortgage as soon as possible.
4. Your client shall register a charge against the property upon completion of the transfer; this shall be to secure his share of the net equity at 45%.

5. The net equity of the property shall be calculated as the value of the property minus the mortgage at the date of the agreement. This currently stands at [*insert redemption figure*], less the costs of sale fixed at 2.5%.
6. Your client can expect to be paid the monies secured by way of charge, upon the occurrence of the first event listed below:

    (a) the youngest child of the family finishing his full-time tertiary education up to the end of the first degree, to include a gap year;
    (b) the death of the applicant;
    (c) the applicant remarrying;
    (d) further order.

7. The events that trigger the payment of your client's money shall not be exercisable without permission of the court while any child of the family in occupation of the property is still a minor, or of full age but receiving full-time tertiary education or training.
8. Your client shall pay all school or university fees and reasonable extras as appearing on the school or university bill. These shall be paid as and when demanded by the school or university. This obligation shall be in respect of both children for the schools they currently attend or any school that the parties agree the children should attend in the future.
9. Your client shall pay child maintenance at the figure assessed by the Child Maintenance Service.
10. Your client shall pay spousal maintenance for our client at the rate of £1,200 per calendar month. Such maintenance shall be paid until the occurrence of the first of the following events:

    (a) the youngest child of the family finishing full-time tertiary education up to the end of the first degree to include a gap year;
    (b) remarriage of the applicant;
    (c) the death of the applicant or respondent.

11. The applicant may apply for an order to extend this term.
12. The spousal maintenance payments shall be varied annually in line with any increase of the Consumer Price Index (CPI).
13. There shall be a 42% pension sharing order in favour of the applicant, and the parties will pay the costs of the trustees for pension sharing implementation equally. This is in line with the pension expert's report.
14. The parties have divided the contents of the family home between them.
15. There shall be a clean break in respect of your client's claims against ours in life and death.
16. There shall be a clean break in respect of our client's claims, save for her income claims which will remain open until expiration of the term. When our client's maintenance comes to an end, she will no longer be able to make an application under the Inheritance (Provision for Family and Dependants) Act 1975, s.2.
17. Each party shall pay their own costs in respect of the financial remedy proceedings. There is a costs order that your client is to pay the costs of divorce. We agreed to cap these costs at £1,500. The costs should be paid within 14 days of the final divorce order being pronounced.
18. There shall be liberty to apply.

### Net effect

The above offer is designed to minimise any disruption to the children, which the parties both agree is their goal. Our client will remain in the family home and we accept that until she is able to release your client from his covenants under the joint mortgage, he is unlikely to be able to purchase another property. He is currently living in rented accommodation, and although he would like to purchase a property this is not likely to be possible until he receives his share of the net equity in the family home.

Your client will receive net equity of 45%. The small departure away from equality is to reflect the money that he withdrew from the parties' joint savings account when he left the family home. This money was used to pay the deposit at the property he currently rents and the first month's rent. He will receive most of the deposit money back when he vacates the property. Save for that one small adjustment, the above offer reflects an equal division of the property and pensions.

You will note from the attached schedule of assets that your client will be left with 30% of his net income after he has paid the school fees and child and spousal maintenance as per the terms of the order. His net income will allow him to pay his rent and reasonable costs of living as per his outgoings schedule.

We believe that the above offer is fair to both the parties as they will both continue to maintain a standard of living which is similar to that enjoyed by them during the marriage. Our client understands that your client wants to purchase a property rather than rent a property; sadly, the current circumstances do not allow for this.

We look forward to receiving a copy of your client's open position.

Yours faithfully

# 7 Draft orders

## 7.1 Introduction

Prior to the introduction of the standard orders by the lead financial judge, various forms of order were used. Now, however, it is universally accepted that the standard orders will form the basis of any orders drawn.

With the advent of the digital portal, the practitioner attending a hearing will usually be asked to email the draft order to the judge for the judge to approve, and then upload it to the portal for the judge to formally approve the order. The approved, sealed order will appear in the portal and parties will receive an email notification that it is available for download.

## 7.2 First directions appointment (First Appointment)

Prior to the First Appointment, you will be complying with the requirements of the Efficiency Statement and the Rules for preparation for the First Appointment. It is helpful, if you are representing the applicant, to prepare a draft order, as far as is possible. Remember that once the brief is delivered to counsel, counsel has conduct of the case from that point onwards and therefore will prepare a draft order.

Matters that are often overlooked and need to be provided for in the draft order at First Appointment are:

1. The requirement that a Form H (Estimate of Costs) must have been not only produced but also discussed with the client.
2. The requirement for the FM5 to be filed before the First Appointment.

The order that is drafted will always deal with preparation for the FDR – updating documentation, bundles and listing. However, the other issues of property valuation, pension reports, whether a medical condition impairs earning capacity etc will vary from case to case. The important points for you to consider are what is to be done and when it is to be done by, considering the mechanism by which an expert will be chosen, the terms of the letter of instruction being agreed and who will pay for any questions to be asked.

Often, if the property value is agreed, the order will record that.

## 7.3 FDR order

The suite of orders has a template for an FDR order, of course, and this is what should be used.

If settlement is reached at the FDR hearing, it is preferable for a full order to be agreed at court, whilst all parties are in the building. For that reason, it would be wise for you to have a rough template ready prior attending to represent your client. Counsel will do this if instructed for the FDR.

If there really is no time for a financial order to be drafted then parties can draw a simplified 'Heads of Agreement' document with the basic points of agreement to be set out and to be finessed in a final order. In this situation, the court will usually list the matter for a short Mention hearing of around 10 minutes that can be vacated if the parties submit a final order.

The final order by consent has to be uploaded within the contested financial remedy portal. It is only where no application has been made that the consented financial remedy portal can be used.

Remember the court cannot make a final order until the conditional divorce order has been pronounced. If you find yourself in that situation, you would either be relying on FPR 2010, rule 29.15 – for the order to be made at the current date but not to take effect until the conditional divorce order has been made – or you will be relying on the jurisdiction per *Rose* v. *Rose*. In *Rose* v. *Rose* [2002] EWCA Civ 208 the parties reached an agreement, and although the judge approved the terms, there was insufficient time to draw up a consent order before the court closed. Nevertheless, it was determined that in expressing his approval of the agreement, the judge was, in effect, making an order in the agreed terms. A *Rose* order is, therefore, by definition, 'one that is final and binding notwithstanding the fact that it still requires perfection and sealing'. See also *G* v. *C* [2020] EWFC B35 (OJ).

## 7.4 Consent order

The suite of orders has a comprehensive final order covering all variations of aspects agreed by the parties.

It is now mandatory for solicitors to lodge a consent order for approval via the myHMCTS Financial Remedies portal. The Form A is subsumed into screens within the system. The documents to be uploaded are:

1. The financial remedies order signed by all parties in either PDF or Word format. Electronic signatures are acceptable.
2. The Form D81 – preferably a joint document but if agreement really cannot be reached, separate Forms D81 can be uploaded for each party.
3. Pension sharing annex(es).

4. Any other document considered necessary for the judge to see. This may be heads of agreement post mediation (provided privilege is waived), a marital agreement – pre nuptial, post nuptial or separation – or an arbitration award.

A court fee is payable (£58 as at 1 May 2024) and is collected via the PBA account of the registered solicitor.

You will receive an email notification of the application being assigned to the judge and then a communication email notification from the portal advising whether the order is approved and when it is available for download. You should check that the date has been inserted by the court into the pension sharing annex to avoid problems with implementation.

If the consent order is prepared at court following a successful FDR hearing, no D81 needs to be filed (FPR 2010, rule 9.26(5)) and no filing fee needs to be paid. It is important, however, that the agreed order is lodged within the case in the contested portal. The consented route cannot be used.

If the consent order is submitted following a successful arbitration, the process is the same as the route for a consented application, with the award being uploaded so as to inform the judge.

## 7.5 Conclusion

In light of standardisation of the orders to be used in financial matters, you should make sure you keep yourself apprised of any changes and use the up-to-date versions of orders. You can inform yourself by subscribing to many free resources – President's View From Chambers; judiciary website; Financial Remedies Journal to name a few.

# 8 Schedule 1 Children Act proceedings

## 8.1 Introduction

This chapter deals with those cases where the parties are not married but there are claims that can be made in respect of the children of the family.

An application can be made to the Family Court for periodical payments for the children, a lump sum order in respect of children's expenses, or the transfer or settlement of property for the benefit of the children.

These applications are usually made between unmarried parents but can be made in respect of a step-parent who was married or in a civil partnership. Bear in mind that those applications can also be made within the context of divorce and dissolution, which is often the preferable forum for them.

An application for periodical payments can also be made by a guardian or special guardian or any person named in a child arrangements order with whom the child is to live.

The court has jurisdiction even if the child lives outside the jurisdiction of England and Wales, as long as one parent lives within the jurisdiction.

## 8.2 Informing the client about the applications

The letter at **Annex 8A** explains to the client the claims that can be made for the benefit of the child. It is assumed that the letter is written to the mother with whom the child resides. As the claims are for the benefit of the child, one parent will be the payer and that person will not make cross-applications.

Although there is no requirement for the parties to enter into a consent order upon reaching an agreement, it is sensible to record any terms in the form of an order and send it to the court for approval in the usual way. As these matters are governed by the Children Act 1989 and not MCA 1973, the court will be more likely to approve any agreements reached by the parties.

The letter explains the mother's right to make applications for maintenance in certain circumstances. Subparagraphs A–E should be carefully selected to ensure that the court has jurisdiction to make maintenance orders instead of or in addition to the CMS.

The Child Support Act 1991 sets out those circumstances where the CMS does not have jurisdiction to make a maintenance assessment:

1. due to a child's age;
2. if one of the parents is outside the jurisdiction;
3. where an application for educational expenses is to be paid;
4. where an application for expenses related to a disability is to be paid;
5. where the maximum assessment has been made, the court will have jurisdiction to make a 'top up' order;
6. where maintenance is sought from a step-parent.

You should ensure that claims can be made before sending the letter to the client, or at least couch the letter in more general terms if the client is unaware of the other parent's financial circumstances.

See further *AB* v. *CD* [2023] EWFC 103, *W* v. *H* [2021] EWFC B63, *Dickinson* v. *Rennie* [2014] EWHC 4306 (Fam), *James* v. *Seymour* [2023] EWHC 844 (Fam).

## 8.3 Making the application

The application has to be made via the financial remedy digital portal. The application form (Form A1) is subsumed into the screens. The claims to be made must be thought through much more carefully than in MCA 1973 applications, as some claims may not be relevant; for example, the applicant may not be able to claim maintenance from the court if the CMS has made an assessment which is not a maximum assessment, unless that application is withdrawn. These applications cannot be used to apply for maintenance through the 'back door'.

Consent applications are also made via the portal.

The application form specifically refers to the jurisdiction of the court to make periodical payments orders and requires the applicant to indicate whether CMS has made a maintenance calculation.

The applicant is required to give details for the children and state where they reside if this is outside England and Wales. This is to establish whether the court has jurisdiction to make the orders requested.

Details of service are straightforward, as are the pages in respect of the MIAM application, which mirror those in the Form A.

The application is signed with a statement of truth, which can be signed by the solicitor on behalf of the client or signed by the client themselves.

The application is made to the Family Court and submitted with a filing fee.

## 8.4 Financial disclosure

Form E1 'Financial Statement for a financial remedy (other than a financial order or financial relief after an overseas divorce or dissolution etc) in the family court or High Court' is available online via HMCTS Form Finder.

You should note that sometimes the parties agree to use the Form E even though it is not specifically designed to be used in a Children Act 1989 Schedule 1 application.

When the timetable from the court is received after the Form A1 is issued, it usually indicates that the parties should complete the financial statement that they believe is best suited for the proceedings. There is therefore some degree of discretion on your part.

The financial statement in the Form E1 is shorter than the Form E but there are many similarities. For example, the first page contains the same warnings and if parties do not give full frank and clear disclosure of their financial and other circumstances then there are likely to be consequences. An application to set aside any order based upon inadequate disclosure may be one of those consequences.

Section 1 requires the applicant to insert personal information about themselves, their residence and details of all children and dependants involved.

Section 1.9 requires the applicant to give details about their own state of health and that of the children if the applicant thinks this should be taken into account. It is good practice to give full information and attach any relevant documentation. The court will direct expert medical evidence if this is necessary, for example, in circumstances where a child has additional financial requirements as a result of disability. It should be noted, as these matters are dealt with under the Children Act 1989, that FPR 2010 and that Part 25 apply but Practice Direction 25C is more relevant in these proceedings than Practice Direction 25B.

This part broadly follows the outline of the Form E as detailed in **Chapter 3**.

## 8.5 Employment

Section 2.1 requires the applicant to indicate if they are employed, self-employed, unemployed or a pensioner. They are then directed to a different section of the financial statement to give further details.

Section 2.2 requires the applicant to complete details of income from employment and mirrors the requirements in the Form E. See commentary in **Chapter 3** for further details.

Section 2.3 requires the applicant to complete details of income from self-employment or partnership and mirrors Form E. See commentary in **Chapter 3** for further details.

Section 3.1 requires details of income from investments; section 3.2 requires details of state benefits; and section 3.3 requires the applicant to disclose any income not disclosed in previous sections. These also mirror the requirements in the Form E. See commentary in **Chapter 3** for further details.

## 8.6 Capital

Section 4.1 requires information to be provided with regard to any interest in property, land or buildings. This mirrors the requirements in the Form E. See commentary in **Chapter 3** for further details.

Sections 4.2 and 4.3 require information about bank accounts and investments. These sections mirror the requirements in the Form E. See commentary in **Chapter 3** for further details.

Section 4.4 requires information in relation to life policies and endowment policies. This mirrors the requirements in the Form E. See commentary in **Chapter 3** for further details.

Section 4.5 requires details of other assets that have been listed. This mirrors the requirements in the Form E. See commentary in **Chapter 3** for further details.

Section 4.6 requires the applicant to outline any liabilities. This mirrors the requirements in the Form E. See commentary in **Chapter 3** for further details.

## 8.7 Income needs

The applicant is required to list their regular expenses and although this section of the Form E1 is different from Form E, it is sensible to use a template schedule of outgoings such as that in **Annex 3C** rather than complete the form at section 5.1. Section 5.2 requires information about the needs of the child.; this is incorporated at **Annex 3C** and further commentary can be found in **Chapter 3**.

## 8.8 Financial resources of the children

This provision is not in the Form E and is specific to an application under Schedule 1 to the Children Act 1989. The court can take into account the financial resources of the children and will do so where appropriate. If the parties agree to use the Form E to disclose their resources, the children's finances should be clearly set out.

The form needs to be signed with the statement of truth and the relevant documents need to be attached with a list of documents (see **Annex 3B**).

## 8.9 Final order

The suite of standard orders has template orders for these types of applications.

## 8.10 Conclusion

Applications under Schedule 1 to the Children Act 1989 are very different from applications for a financial order under the MCA 1973 or the Civil Partnership Act 2004. You should be careful not to dabble in these proceedings without first having a clear understanding of the jurisdictional issues and the limited orders that the court will make in these proceedings, particularly the types of orders that can and cannot be made.

# Annex 8A

## First letter to applicant in Schedule 1 Children Act claim

Dear [*name of client*]

Thank you for coming to see me with regard to the breakdown of your relationship. As you have [a child/children] together you can make financial applications against [*name of other parent*] for the child(ren)'s benefit.

[I have written to you separately about using non-court dispute resolution. If you and [*name of other parent*] have decided to go to mediation, use collaborative law or arbitration, then you do not need to make financial claims at Court straight away. Hopefully, you will be able to come to an agreement about your financial matters. If that is the case you will not need to make an application for the Court to resolve matters.]

It would be sensible, however, to turn the agreement into a draft consent order which is sent to the Court to confirm the terms of settlement.

You can make the following claims against [*name of other parent*] in respect of [*name(s) of child(ren)*].

### Property claims

It is possible for you to make a claim for the Court to transfer or settle property on you or [*name(s) of child(ren)*]. The Court will make this order if it is for the benefit of [*name(s) of child(ren)*].

You should be aware that the Court will only order property to be available while [*name(s) of child(ren)*] [is/are] under the age of 18. Ultimately, the other parent's share will return to them. Occasionally the Court will extend that period until [*name(s) of child(ren)*] have finished full-time tertiary education. This is usually when the children finish their first degree.

The Court will not make an order to transfer a property to [*name(s) of child(ren)*] outright, the property will always revert back to [*name of other parent*].

### Capital orders

The Court can make lump sum orders for expenses that relate to [*name(s) of child(ren)*]. This could be an order for a one-off payment or an order for a series of payments over a period of time. The structure of the payment will depend on the circumstances of the case. It can also be for the costs incurred for impending birth of the child.

### Income orders

The Court may have the power to make income orders for the benefit of the child(ren) of the family.

A. [You will first need to make an application to the Child Maintenance Service to get a maintenance assessment. Please do this as soon as possible.

   If the Child Maintenance Service assesses [*name of other parent*] to pay the maximum sum, the Court will then have the ability to assess additional maintenance for [*name(s) of child(ren)*].]

OR

B. [As [*name*] lives in [a country outside England and Wales] the Court is able to make a maintenance order.]

OR

C. [As [*name(s) of child(ren)*] [is/are] in fee-paying schools, the Court can order [*name of other parent*] to pay these educational expenses.]

OR

D. [As [*name(s) of child(ren)*] [is/are] disabled the Court can order [*name of other parent*] to pay any expenses related to the disability.]

OR

E. [As [*name of step-parent*] is a step-parent [he/she] can be made to pay maintenance by the Court rather than via the Child Maintenance Service.]

There is a question mark over whether the court can make an order if each of you has equal care of your child/children and we would need to discuss this further.

Payments can be made to you for [*name(s) of child(ren)*]'s benefit or to them directly. These payments should be for [*name(s) of child(ren)*]'s benefit although this can include some of your expenses as their primary carer.

An order will usually be made until the [child(ren)] reach[es] the age of 17. Sometimes the Court will extend these payments beyond [*name(s) of child(ren)*]'s 18th birthday.

## Financial support now

The Court can make an order for [*name of other parent*] to pay maintenance for [*name of child(ren)*].

An interim order can include any claim for your legal costs to make the application.

## Costs orders

It is possible to get a costs order in these proceedings, but this will be a matter for the Judge to decide. We will ensure that we advise you on these matters if litigation starts.

I hope you understand the orders that the Court is able to make. If you have any questions or queries please do not hesitate to contact me.

Yours sincerely